BRITISH
FOODBIBLE

BRITISH
FOODBIBLE

THE BEST OF BRITISH FOOD

Bath • New York • Singapore • Hong Kong • Cologne • Delhi
Melbourne • Amsterdam • Johannesburg • Shenzhen

This edition published in 2012

Parragon
Queen Street House
4 Queen Street
Bath BA1 1HE, UK
www.parragon.com

ISBN: 978-1-4454-9366-4

Printed in China

New photography by Mike Cooper
New home economy by Lincoln Jefferson
Edited by Fiona Biggs
Recipes by Pamela Gwyther
Introduction by Beverly LeBlanc

Notes for the Reader
This book uses both metric and imperial measurements. Follow the same units of measurement throughout; do not mix metric and imperial. All spoon measurements are level: teaspoons are assumed to be 5 ml, and tablespoons are assumed to be 15 ml. Unless otherwise stated, milk is assumed to be full fat, eggs and individual vegetables are medium, and pepper is freshly ground black pepper. Unless otherwise stated, all root vegetables should be washed in plain water and peeled prior to using.

For best results, use a food thermometer when cooking meat and poultry – check the latest government guidelines for current advice.

Garnishes, decorations and serving suggestions are all optional and not necessarily included in the recipe ingredients or method.

The times given are an approximate guide only. Preparation times differ according to the techniques used by different people and the cooking times may also vary from those given. Optional ingredients, variations or serving suggestions have not been included in the time calculations.

Recipes using raw or very lightly cooked eggs should be avoided by infants, the elderly, pregnant women, convalescents and anyone suffering from an illness. Pregnant and breastfeeding women are advised to avoid eating peanuts and peanut products. Sufferers from nut allergies should be aware that some of the ready-made ingredients used in the recipes in this book may contain nuts. Always check the packaging before use.

Picture acknowledgements
The publisher would like to thank the following for permission to reproduce copyright material:
Front cover images: Fish and chips © Caraccio, Stephen/the food passionates/Corbis, Union Jack © Paul Hardy/Corbis
P8–9, 12, 14, 15 (x3), 17, 18, 20–21, 42–43, 66–67, 92–93, 116–117, 140–141, 168–169, 196–197: Various © Getty Images

Contents

Introduction   8
1 The Big Breakfast   20

Apple & Spice Porridge   22

Classic Orange Marmalade & Toast   24

The Full English   26

Bacon Butties   28

Laverbread   30

Ways with Eggs   32

Potato Cakes   36

Kippers   38

Kedgeree   40

2 Light Bites   42

Broccoli & Stilton Soup   44

Leek & Potato Soup   46

Scotch Broth   48

Cullen Skink   50

Classic Sandwich Selection   52

Ploughman's with Chutney   54

Welsh Rarebit   56

Pan Haggerty   58

Ham & Egg Pie   60

Cornish Pasties   62

Pork & Apple Pies   64

3 Classic Pub Grub   66

Prawn Cocktail   68

Coronation Chicken   70

Beef Stew with Herb Dumplings   72

Yorkshire Puddings   74

Steak & Kidney Pie   76

Irish Stew   78

Pork Hot Pot   80

Braised Lamb Shanks   82

Gammon Steaks with Fried Egg & Chips   84

Sausage & Mash   86

Fisherman's Pie 88

Vegetable Toad-In-The-Hole 90

4 Something Special 92

Beef Wellington 94

Roast Gammon 96

Game Pie 98

Venison Casserole 100

Roast Turkey with Two Stuffings 102

Accompaniments 104

Boned & Stuffed Roast Duck 106

Poached Salmon with Hollandaise Sauce 108

Griddled Scallops with Crispy Leeks 110

Garlic & Herb Dublin Bay Prawns 112

Mixed Nut Roast with Cranberry
  & Red Wine Sauce 114

5 Weekend Wonders 116

Roast Beef 118

Roast Leg Of Lamb 120

Shepherd's Pie 122

Toad-In-The-Hole 124

Roast Pork with Crackling 126

Chicken, Mushroom & Tarragon Pie 128

Roast Chicken 130

Fish & Chips 132

Fish Cakes 134

Star-Gazy Pie 136

Perfect Macaroni Cheese 138

6 Vegetables & Sides 140

Perfect Roast Potatoes 142

Champ 144

Honeyed Parsnips 146

Cauliflower Cheese 148

Brussels Sprouts with Buttered Chestnuts 150

Ways with Mushrooms 152

Bubble & Squeak 154

Neeps & Tatties	156
Braised Red Cabbage	158
Roasted Onions	160
Roasted Root Vegetables	162
Asparagus with Melted Butter	164
Garden Salads & Herbs	166

7 Teatime Treats — 168

Victoria Sponge Cake	170
Date & Walnut Teabread	172
Gingerbread	174
Battenberg Cake	176
Shortbread	178
Scones	180
Tea Cakes	182
Muffins	184
Crumpets	186
Barm Brack	188
Irish Soda Bread	190
Raspberry Jam	192
Lemon Curd	194

8 Puddings — 196

Apple Pie	198
Lemon Meringue Pie	200
Treacle Tart	202
Rhubarb Crumble	204
Spotted Dick & Custard	206
Baked Rice Pudding	208
Bread & Butter Pudding	210
Jam Roly-Poly	212
Steamed Syrup Sponge	214
Summer Pudding	216
Classic Sherry Trifle	218
Index	220
Conversion Charts	224

Introduction

Traditional home cooking from England, Wales, Scotland and Northern Ireland has never been totally forgotten, although it has often had to play second fiddle to many food fads over the years. Fortunately, it is now enjoying a revival and cooks everywhere are remembering the joys of eating British food. It is hearty, often filling and, most important of all, flavoursome. This is why many of the recipes in this collection have been passed down over the years through the generations.

Quality, fresh ingredients are the backbone of British cooking. British cooks have almost always been blessed with great variety and choice, and the recipes in this collection reflect this abundance. Enjoy savouring the flavours of Britain.

What is British Food?

British food is both simple and sophisticated, but many traditional favourites recall harsher times. Hotpots, stews, shepherd's pie and cottage pie, for example, are inexpensive dishes intended to fill up farm or factory workers, while leaving the cook free to get on with other chores.

British food has always had something to satisfy everyone and food fashions have never stood still, many coming full circle today. In the nineteenth century, for example, Scottish servants protested against being fed oysters every evening, as the molluscs were one of the cheapest ingredients available. Subsequently, oysters commanded premium prices because of their scarcity, but the introduction of oyster farming has made them affordable again.

After foreign travel was embraced in the 1960s it became faddish to favour one foreign cuisine after another, often leaving traditional British food off menus. The availability of low-cost convenience food also had a detrimental effect. At last, however, British food is enjoying a revival, with many cooks returning to their culinary roots. Celebrity chefs have rekindled interest in preparing delicious home-cooked meals, and we are discovering the joys of cooking using seasonal, local ingredients. New cooks are also learning a basic truth that was second nature to their great-grandparents – seasonal ingredients are best and cheapest. For example, Brussels sprouts reach their flavour peak in the winter months and strawberries are at their most luscious and plentiful in the summer. Eating in tune with the seasons goes hand in hand with traditional British cooking – winter root vegetables are the staple of warming stews and casseroles, while summer meals tend to be lighter, with greater emphasis on fresh salad items and fruits. Subscribing to a vegetable box scheme will give you a good idea of which foods are seasonal when.

The great British food revival is also being promoted by a new generation of professional chefs. These enthusiastic cooks are breathing fresh life into humdrum and mediocre pub kitchens. Gastropubs rival traditional restaurants as the places to go for good, but relaxed, dining. Traditional pub favourites – prawn cocktail, steak and kidney pie, beef stew with dumplings, and sausages and mash, to name a few – are back on the menu, now sitting comfortably alongside the more exotic stir-fries and curries that have become part of our culinary landscape.

Consumers are also playing their part in the exciting food revival. Increased concern over the environmental costs of producing and transporting fresh produce means that people want to know where their food comes from and how it has been produced. There is also a widening appreciation of organic food, boosting farmers' markets, delicatessens and specialist food shops.

Celebrating with British Food

Just as eating seasonally gives a sense of the passage of time, many British dishes are closely linked with secular and religious celebrations throughout the year. In Scotland, for example, where the new year is ushered in with Hogmanay, the first-footer arrives with a piece of coal, bread and whisky, representing mankind's need for warmth, food and comfort. On 25 January, no Burns Night dinner in honour of the Scottish poet is complete without a generous serving of haggis, neeps and tatties.

Since medieval times, when cream, eggs and milk were forbidden during Lent, pancakes have been served on Shrove Tuesday to use up supplies in the larder before fasting begins the next day, Ash Wednesday. Pancake-tossing races are still enjoyed in many communities.

Mothering Sunday also has its origins in medieval times, not as a celebration of motherhood, but rather as a mid-Lenten break, when church rules required priests and lay people to return to their mother church for worship. As this eventually evolved into a day of feasting, simnel cake became part of the celebrations, and serving girls were given a day off by their employers to visit their mothers, bringing with them a simnel cake baked with the employer's ingredients. The dense fruitcake, as baked today, contains a layer of rich marzipan through the centre and another layer of marzipan on the top, with eleven marzipan balls, representing Jesus' disciples, minus Judas, arranged around the edge. Traditionally, simnel cake isn't eaten until Easter Day, when the Lenten prohibition on eating anything but the plainest food is lifted.

Many foods are associated with the Easter season. Hot cross buns, lightly spiced and topped with dough crosses, are a Good Friday tradition. Since ancient times, eggs have been a symbol of continuing life, and brightly dyed and decorated hard-boiled Easter eggs have evolved out of that belief, with egg-rolling races being a symbolic celebration of the returning sun and spring. (It was said that the first boy and girl to get their eggs to the bottom of a hill would marry each other, providing an added incentive, for some, to win the race.) For the actual Easter day meal, spring food takes pride of place, and roast lamb with seasonal herbs, such as mint and parsley, is always a popular choice for the celebratory lunch. Baked custards were once a regular part of the Easter feast, celebrating the end of the six-week prohibition on eggs and cream.

As spring gives way to summer, tennis at the All-England Lawn Tennis and Croquet Club, in Wimbledon, just wouldn't seem complete without bowls of juicy strawberries and cream. Summer pudding, with its bread casing and rich, red interior, isn't part of any specific holiday observances, simply a timely celebration of the season's glorious soft fruit.

When the weather cools and it's time to remember Guy Fawkes on the fifth of November, Bonfire Night parties demand warming food – this often includes hot, spiced cider, jacket potatoes and parkin, a sticky ginger cake from northern England. Halloween, which derives from

the religious observance of All Hallows' Eve on the last night of October, is now frequently combined with Bonfire Night celebrations, adding toffee apples and barm brack from Ulster to the menu.

As British cooks' attentions turn towards Christmas, Stir-up Sunday, the second Sunday in Advent, is the traditional time to make the Christmas pudding, with each family member giving the thick batter a stir. In the West Country and throughout the south-east, with the many apple orchards, wassailing is a long-established tradition on Christmas Eve, or St Stephen's feast day (Boxing Day). Throughout British history, the Christmas Day feast has been the peak of the culinary year. Turkey or goose might provide the main course for many families today, but over the centuries boars'

heads, venison, peacocks and roast beef have all been favoured. Mince pies have had a part in the festivities since Elizabethan times.

The Best of British

Regional dishes, reflecting local geography and socio-economic history, add to the joy of the British culinary tradition. Wherever you travel, you will find delicious specialities made with local ingredients.

East Anglia

The gentle, undulating farmlands of East Anglia, which stretch as far as the eye can see across low-lying, distant horizons, combined with a relatively dry climate, provide much of our soft fruit, wheat, barley, golden rape, sugar beet, salad greens and apples.

This is also where a large proportion of the nation's poultry is raised, including the tender Norfolk Bronze turkey that graces many Christmas tables.

Some of the finest shellfish, including cockles, crabs, mussels, oysters, prawns, shrimp and whelks, come from here, along with cod, haddock, plaice, sole and turbot. Cromer crabs, from Norfolk, are heavy for their small size, which instantly lets you know they are packed with succulent meat. Herring have always been landed here, and small smokers produce kippers and bloaters to keep an ancient tradition alive.

The Midlands

Once Britain's industrial powerhouse, today the Midlands is a centre of agricultural activity. Hereford beef is enjoyed all over the country, and the red soil in parts of the region is ideal for apple and pear orchards

and soft fruit, stone fruit and vegetables in abundance. When the Vale of Evesham's asparagus appears in markets, try it dipped in melted butter to appreciate the fine flavour.

Blue Stilton, labelled 'the king of British cheeses', must be produced within the boundaries of Derbyshire, Leicestershire and Nottinghamshire. Its international reputation, however, often overshadows the region's other noteworthy cheeses – Cheshire, Sage Derby, Red Leicester and Shropshire Blue.

The picturesque market town of Melton Mowbray is home to the uniquely British, eponymous pork pie, with its crisp hot-water crust and spiced filling.

Worcestershire sauce, one of the world's favourite savoury flavourings, began life in the 1830s, the result of a mistake by two chemists, Mr Lea and Mr Perrins.

The North

Food from this vast region, stretching from the Midlands north to the Scottish Borders, is traditionally hearty and filling. Lancashire hotpot, a one-pot dish of lamb chops and root vegetables, was once only considered suitable for family meals, but now has pride of place on many pub and restaurant menus. For another taste of no-frills northern cooking, try toad in the hole, or its vegetable counterpart. And, of course, there is its cousin, Yorkshire pudding, the light, fluffy baked batter dish served alongside roast beef that was once a first course intended to fill up diners so less meat was required. Northumberland's pan haggerty, a large fried potato cake cooked with onions and Cheddar cheese, is still a delicious and filling way to start a meal.

The northern cook's reputation for frugality can still be glimpsed today when tripe and onions are served. Vast grasslands, much on rugged terrain, support cattle and sheep, providing meat as well as excellent dairy products. Northern butchers pride themselves on their black puddings, as well as other offal preparations, and their succulent meat pies, sold hot for eating on the spot or taking away. Dry-cured York ham, with its distinctive golden crumb coating, must be smoked over oak within two miles of the city of York if it is to be considered authentic. On the other side of the Pennines, the mounded coils of the unique Cumberland sausage are instantly recognizable in butcher's-shop windows.

The long tradition of fishing along both coasts today faces shrinking stocks and economic pressure, but fishermen still provide herring, whitefish and shellfish. The tiny brown shrimp and cockles that come from Morecambe Bay are considered a delicacy. Freshwater char, a fish that is similar to salmon in taste and texture, is a spring favourite around Lake Windermere, in the Lake District.

Crumbly white Lancashire cheese, with its salty flavour, is a regional favourite. Try a slice of unpasteurized Lancashire with an Eccles cake (spiced currants encased in puff pastry) for an intriguing and delicious end to a meal. Other regional cheeses worth looking for include Cotherstone and Wensleydale – wonderful eaten with fruit chutney.

Northern Ireland

There is more to the Northern Irish diet than just potatoes, although it's rare to eat a meal here without them. Cultivated since the 1600s, when they were introduced from the New World, potatoes were a subsistence crop in hard times, but today they take their place alongside simple but delicious lamb, pork, beef and plenty of seafood dishes.

Boom times in Belfast kindled a renewed interest in traditional food and cooking, with artisan producers and cooks striving to put the region on Britain's culinary map. Yet, traditional favourites, such as Irish stew, are not forgotten. This one-pot meal typifies the region's cooking at its best. Champ – mashed potatoes with spring onions, flavoured with butter and herbs – is another example of simple everyday fare that now has pride of place on many a restaurant menu.

Northern Irish pig farmers provide all of Britain with bacon, both smoked and green, as well as flavoured with various cures. The Ulster fry is a veritable breakfast masterpiece, with bacon, eggs, sausage, black and white pudding, mushrooms and tomatoes served up with moist potato farls.

River fishing is a popular sport, and cooks benefit from it with a good supply of trout, salmon, perch and pike. Fishing off the coast also provides cod, plaice and skate, as well as fresh prawns and oysters.

Northern Ireland has a tradition of home baking, and Irish soda bread has always been the cook's favourite because it is so quick to mix and bake. Barm brack, a dry spiced fruit bread, is served in thick slices smothered with creamy butter. Traditionally made for the Halloween festivities, it was customary to mix items such as coins, wedding rings, bits of clean rag and twigs into the dough – these were believed to have a significance for the future of the person taking the slice that contained any of them. These days, in the interests of health and safety, the added extras are omitted.

Scotland

From the gentle, rolling Borders to the soaring Highlands and the Islands, Scotland yields a bountiful selection of ingredients that can delight any cook. Scottish smoked salmon, Highland cattle, game and luscious ruby raspberries are valued by cooks throughout Britain. Yet, despite this abundance of wonderful foods, perhaps the country's best-known 'ingredients' are the numerous Scotch whiskies that are savoured worldwide.

Many fish are caught in Scotland's lochs, rivers and surrounding waters, but salmon and herring are the best known. Both have an oily flesh that lends itself to hot and cold smoking – Arbroath smokies and kippers are examples of Scottish smoked herring. Smoked haddock is an essential ingredient in cullen skink, a hearty fish and potato soup.

Aberdeen Angus, a popular breed of cattle that endures the harsh grazing conditions of northern Scotland, is

highly valued in top kitchens everywhere. Deer are also adept at surviving in the Highlands, and the lean meat is ideal for venison casserole. Feathered game and wild hare are also popular, and game pie is a regular feature on menus after the 'Glorious Twelfth' of August when the grouse season opens. Haggis, an acquired taste and a uniquely Scottish favourite, is traditionally served with neeps and tatties (turnips with mashed potatoes).

Scotland also has a long tradition of cheese-making. Lanark Blue, made from sheep's milk, has a tangy flavour. Dunlop is the Scottish version of Cheddar, and Caboc is a very rich, soft cheese rolled in oatmeal.

London and the South

Despite the domination of bustling London and densely populated commuter towns, the Home Counties and the south-east of England contain a great deal of agricultural land, supplying the capital and the rest of the country with orchard fruit, soft fruit, vegetables, meat and dairy products. Wine and beer producers are also established in the region.

Many of Britain's favourite eponymous ingredients, products and dishes come from this region: Aylesbury duck, Chelsea buns, Eton mess, Oxford marmalade, Sussex pond pudding and Whitstable oysters.

Kent, with its moist climate and rich soil, is known as the 'garden of England'. Many varieties of apples and pears, hops and cob nuts grow here whilst in Hampshire, the New Forest mushrooms are a seasonal delicacy.

Fishmongers here have plenty to offer from the English Channel as it winds southward from the Thames Estuary. Capture the flavour of a seaside holiday with fish and chips, which followed the cockney trail when they left London.

London's contributions to Britain's culinary history are unmistakable. Since medieval times, chefs in the capital's public eating houses (*publica coquina*) have been setting the standards that are eventually adopted throughout the country. London's docks are also where many culinary treasures of the world, such as spices, entered Britain, adding extra flavour to home-grown produce. Chefs have always been ready to try new ingredients and dishes, which is why Britain has such a rich, constantly evolving cuisine.

Wales

When you think of Wales it is impossible not to think of the flocks of lamb in the harsh, mountainous landscape dotted with hill farms. The grazing provides what is probably the best-flavoured lamb in the world.

Welsh food is traditionally simple, with plenty of richness added by butter, cheese and cream. For a taste of Wales, start with leek and potato soup, showcasing the iconic vegetable symbol of Wales, followed by roast leg of lamb with roast potatoes. Seaweed is a regional delicacy from around the Gower Peninsula. Laverbread – purple laver seaweed picked from the rocks and cooked until it becomes a dark green, spinach-like mass, then rolled in oatmeal and fried – has never fallen out of favour. It can be an acquired taste, but complements sizzling bacon for a traditional breakfast.

The West Country

West Country cooks are literally spoilt for choice. Abundant orchards provide apples for eating, baking and for making cider, the region's signature drink.

Cheddar, the world's favourite cheese, has been made in Somerset since the twelfth century. Other notable cheeses include Double and Single Gloucester, Devon Garland and Cornish Yarg. The West Country is the only area to produce that rich and indulgent tea-time treat, clotted cream.

Wiltshire has a long tradition of pig farming – the once almost-extinct Gloucester Old Spot pigs, with tender, succulent meat, are raised here.

Cornish pasties, originally baked as an edible lunchbox for tin miners, remain a popular lunch or snack with holidaymakers and locals alike.

The picturesque coastline yields excellent seafood. Daily catches include mackerel, monkfish, John Dory, sea bass and fine flatfish, along with crabs, lobsters and scallops. The extraordinary looking star-gazy pie, made with sardines, was invented here. Freshwater fish, such as salmon, are also popular and potted crab is a regular feature on local pub and restaurant menus.

The region's seafaring history made it a gateway for exotic spices, so ginger and saffron are often used in baked goods, such as saffron cakes.

BRITISH SEASONAL FOOD
Use this handy guide to savour the best of the seasons with British ingredients. Here's what to look for each month:

JANUARY	Jerusalem artichokes, beetroot, Brussels sprouts, partridges, pheasants, wild duck, scallops
FEBRUARY	Carrots, cauliflower, celeriac, pork, veal, halibut, mussels, oysters, scallops
MARCH	Broccoli, cucumbers, kale, watercress, cooking and dessert apples, pears, salmon, salmon trout, skate
APRIL	Chinese leaves, cucumbers, lettuce, mint, parsley, radishes, spring onions, tomatoes, brill, mackerel, oysters, pork
MAY	Asparagus, endive, peppers, peas, spring onions, apricots, gooseberries, strawberries, crab, lobster, turbot, spring lamb
JUNE	Globe artichokes, asparagus, broad and kidney beans, marrows, new potatoes, black/redcurrants, cherries, loganberries, plums, raspberries, strawberries, mullet, plaice, spring lamb, pork
JULY	Celery, courgettes, endive, greengages, mulberries, peaches, strawberries, brill, halibut, lobster, mullet, whitebait, venison
AUGUST	Calabrese broccoli, pumpkin, radishes, sweetcorn, tomatoes, turnips, damsons, gooseberries, greengages, plums, raspberries, rhubarb, strawberries, haddock, hake, trout, turbot, grouse, venison
SEPTEMBER	Beetroots, parsnips, maincrop potatoes, swedes, sweetcorn, tomatoes, elderberries, lobster, pike, hare, partridge, wild duck
OCTOBER	Celeriac, turnips, cooking and dessert apples, blackberries, black/redcurrants, crab apples, chestnuts, medlars, quinces, strawberries, dab, mussels, oysters, beef, pheasant, wild duck
NOVEMBER	Jerusalem artichokes, carrots, kale, leeks, quinces, scallops, rabbit, turkey
DECEMBER	Brussels sprouts, cauliflower, swedes, watercress, cooking and dessert apples, chestnuts, halibut, herring, pike, skate, turkey, venison

Chapter 1
The Big Breakfast

Apple & Spice Porridge

Serves 4

ingredients
- 600 ml/1 pint milk or water
- 1 tsp salt
- 115 g/4 oz medium rolled porridge oats
- 2 large apples
- ½ tsp ground mixed spice
- honey (optional), to serve

1 Put the milk in a saucepan and bring to the boil. Add the salt and sprinkle in the oats, stirring constantly. Reduce the heat to low and leave to simmer for 10 minutes, stirring occasionally.

2 Meanwhile, halve, core and grate the apples. When the porridge is creamy and much of the liquid has evaporated, stir in the grated apple and mixed spice. Spoon into bowls and drizzle with the honey, if using.

Classic Orange Marmalade
& Toast

Makes about 4.5 kg/10 lb

ingredients
- 1.5 kg/3 lb 5 oz Seville oranges, scrubbed
- juice from 2 large lemons
- 3.4 litres/6 pints water
- 2.7 kg/6 lb preserving sugar
- thick slices of white or brown bread, to serve

1 Cut the oranges in half and squeeze out all the juice. Scoop out all the pips from the orange shells and tie them up in a small piece of muslin. Slice the peel into small chunks or strips and place in a preserving pan together with the orange and lemon juice and water. Add the bag of pips.

2 Simmer gently for 1½ hours, or until the peel is very soft and the liquid has reduced by half. Remove the bag of pips, carefully squeezing to remove any juice. Add the sugar and heat, stirring, until the sugar has completely dissolved.

3 Bring to the boil and boil rapidly for about 15 minutes, or until the setting point is reached. Test if it is set by using a sugar thermometer. When it reads 105°C/221°F it is at a good setting point.

4 Leave to cool slightly, then pot into warmed sterilized jars and cover the tops with waxed discs. When completely cold, cover with cellophane or lids, label and store in a cool place.

5 To serve, toast the bread on both sides under a medium grill or in a toaster. Spread thickly with the marmalade.

The Full English

Serves 1

ingredients
- 2 good-quality pork sausages
- 2–3 smoked back bacon rashers
- 2 eggs
- 1 slice 2-day-old wholemeal bread (optional)
- 1 large tomato, halved
- 2–3 mushrooms
- vegetable oil, for frying and drizzling
- salt and pepper

1 Place the sausages under a hot grill and grill for about 15–20 minutes, turning frequently, until they are well browned.

2 Meanwhile, place the bacon rashers in a dry frying pan and fry for 2–4 minutes on each side, depending on how crisp you like your bacon. Remove from the frying pan, leaving all the excess bacon fat, and keep the bacon warm. The frying pan can then be used to fry the eggs.

3 Alternatively, use the delicious bacon fat to make fried bread. Heat the frying pan and place the bread in the fat. Cook for 1–2 minutes on one side, then turn over and repeat. Do not cook too quickly or the bread will burn.

4 Place the tomato halves under the hot grill with the sausages. Drizzle with a little oil, season to taste with salt and pepper and grill for 3–4 minutes.

5 Grill the mushrooms with the tomatoes or fry them quickly in the frying pan with a little extra oil added.

6 Arrange the sausages, bacon, eggs, fried bread, tomatoes and mushrooms on a large hot platter and serve immediately.

Bacon Butties

Serves 1

ingredients
- 2 smoked bacon rashers
- 15 g/½ oz butter, softened
- 2 thick slices of white or brown bread
- 1 tomato, sliced (optional)
- sauce of choice (brown sauce, tomato ketchup or mustard)
- pepper

1 Cut the rashers of bacon in half so that you have 2 pieces of back bacon and 2 pieces of streaky bacon.

2 Place the bacon under a hot grill and grill, turning frequently, until the bacon is cooked and as crisp as you like it.

3 Meanwhile, butter the bread slices. Place 2 pieces of bacon on one slice of bread and season with a grinding of pepper. Add the tomato, if using, and the sauce. Top with the remaining bacon and the other slice of bread and eat immediately.

Laverbread

Serves 4

ingredients
- 4 tbsp prepared laver
- 2 tbsp fine oatmeal
- 2 tbsp bacon fat or vegetable oil

to serve
- 8 bacon rashers
- 4 tomatoes, halved
- vegetable oil, for drizzling
- salt and pepper

1 Mix the laver with enough oatmeal to make it sufficiently firm to allow you to shape the mixture into four small round cakes.

2 Place the bacon rashers in a dry frying pan and fry for 2–4 minutes on each side, depending on how crisp you like your bacon. Remove from the frying pan, leaving all the excess bacon fat, and keep the bacon warm. The frying pan can then be used to fry the laver bread.

3 Heat the bacon fat in the frying pan and fry the laver bread cakes for 4–5 minutes until nicely browned on one side. Turn over and repeat until cooked through.

4 Meanwhile, preheat the grill to high. Place the tomato halves under the grill, drizzle with a little oil and season to taste with salt and pepper before grilling for 3–4 minutes.

5 Serve the laverbread immediately with the fried bacon and grilled tomatoes.

Ways with Eggs

Eggs are for many people the number one comfort food, and if your happiest childhood memories include boiled eggs and soldiers, you're probably one of them. Eggs are highly nutritious and very quick to prepare, and can be cooked in so many different ways, from boiling and frying to scrambling, poaching and baking, that you don't have to keep them just for breakfast, but can enjoy them for a light lunch or supper or as a hearty snack.

Boiling

You will need a saucepan large enough to cook the number of eggs required, but not so large that the eggs can move around too freely and crack. It is a good idea to have the eggs at room temperature to prevent cracking. Bring the water to a gentle simmer and lower the eggs in using a long-handled spoon. Simmer for 3–4 minutes for soft-boiled, 5–6 for medium-boiled and 10 minutes for hard-boiled. If you are serving hard-boiled eggs cold, always run them under cold water immediately after they are cooked to prevent a black line forming around the yolk.

Scrambling

Allow 2 eggs per person and beat them gently in a basin with a little salt and pepper. Melt 15 g/½ oz butter in a saucepan over a low heat, pour in the beaten eggs and stir gently using a wooden spoon. The egg will start to set on the base of the pan, so lift it away from the base until all the egg is starting to look creamy. Remove from the heat and continue to stir until it does not look wet any more. Serve quickly as you do not want to have rubbery scrambled eggs.

Ways with Eggs

Poaching

You need a small shallow pan (a small frying pan is ideal) and really fresh eggs for this method. Heat enough water to cover the eggs and break 1 egg into a cup. When the water is at a gentle simmer, carefully pour in the egg and allow the white to coagulate around the yolk. Add another egg. Poach for 2–3 minutes if you like a soft yolk or for 4–5 minutes for a firmer egg. Remove from the pan using a slotted spoon, drain quickly on kitchen paper and serve immediately.

Baking

Baked eggs are a simple and delicious way to feed large numbers. Preheat the oven to 190°C/375°F/Gas Mark 5. Generously butter a number of small ramekins and break 1 egg into each dish. Season well with salt and pepper and spoon over 1 tablespoon of single cream. Place the dishes in a roasting tin with enough hot water to come halfway up the sides of the dishes and bake in the preheated oven for 15 minutes for a soft egg and 18–20 minutes for a firmer egg.

Frying

The best way to fry an egg is in the same frying pan in which you have just fried some bacon. This way you can baste your egg with the delicious bacon fat. Otherwise, take 1 tablespoon of oil or 15 g/½ oz butter and heat in a small frying pan over a medium heat. Break the egg into the frying pan (if you are a beginner it might be wise to break the egg into a cup or ramekin first). Fry for a few seconds until the white sets, then baste with the fat to make sure it is evenly cooked with the white completely set and the yolk still soft in the centre. Remove the egg from the pan using a wooden spatula and leave it to rest on a piece of kitchen paper for a second to absorb any excess fat. Serve immediately.

Potato Cakes

Serves 8–10

ingredients

- 550 g/1 lb 4 oz floury potatoes, such as King Edward, Maris Piper or Desirée, peeled and cut into chunks
- 25 g/1 oz butter, plus extra to serve
- 1 egg (optional)
- 115 g/4 oz plain flour
- oil, for greasing
- salt and pepper

1 Bring a large saucepan of lightly salted water to the boil, add the potatoes and cook for 15–20 minutes. Drain well and mash with a potato masher until smooth. Season with salt and pepper and add the butter. Mix in the egg, if using.

2 Turn out the mixture into a large mixing bowl and add enough of the flour to make a light dough. Work quickly, as you do not want the potato to cool too much.

3 Place the dough on a lightly floured surface and roll out carefully to a thickness of 5 mm/¼ inch. Using a 6-cm/2½-inch pastry cutter, cut the dough into rounds.

4 Grease a griddle or heavy-based frying pan with a little oil and heat. Slip the cakes onto the griddle in batches and cook for 4–5 minutes on each side until they are golden brown.

5 Keep the cooked cakes warm until ready to serve, then serve on warmed plates with lots of fresh butter.

Kippers

Serves 1

ingredients
- 1 kipper
- knob of butter
- pepper
- buttered brown bread and lemon
  wedges, to serve

1 Place the kipper in a frying pan and cover with water.

2 Bring to the boil, then reduce the heat, cover and simmer gently for about 5 minutes.

3 Remove the kipper from the pan, drain on kitchen paper and place on a warmed plate with a knob of butter on top and some pepper to taste.

4 Serve immediately with the bread and a squeeze of lemon juice.

Kedgeree

Serves 4

ingredients

- 450 g/1 lb undyed smoked haddock, skinned
- 2 tbsp olive oil
- 1 onion, finely chopped
- 1 tsp mild curry paste
- 175 g/6 oz long-grain rice
- 55 g/2 oz butter
- 3 hard-boiled eggs
- salt and pepper
- 2 tbsp chopped fresh parsley, to garnish

1 Place the fish in a large saucepan and cover with water. Bring the water to the boil, then reduce to a simmer and poach the fish for 8–10 minutes until it flakes easily. Remove the fish and keep warm, reserving the water in a jug or bowl.

2 Put the oil in the pan, add the onion and gently soften for about 4 minutes. Stir in the curry paste and add the rice.

3 Measure 600 ml/1 pint of the haddock water and return to the pan. Bring to a simmer, cover and cook for 10–12 minutes until the rice is tender and the water has been absorbed. Season to taste with salt and pepper.

4 Flake the fish and add to the pan with the butter. Stir very gently over a low heat until the butter has melted. Chop 2 of the hard-boiled eggs and add to the pan.

5 Turn the kedgeree into a serving dish, slice the remaining egg and use to garnish. Scatter the parsley over the kedgeree and serve immediately.

Chapter 2
Light Bites

Broccoli & Stilton Soup

Serves 4

ingredients

- 50 g/1¾ oz butter
- 2 onions, chopped
- 1 potato, peeled and diced
- 1 litre/1¾ pints hot vegetable stock or chicken stock
- 1 broccoli crown, broken into small florets
- 200 ml/7 fl oz double cream
- 200 g/7 oz Stilton or other firm blue cheese, crumbled
- 4 slices of French bread, toasted
- pepper
- 10 g/¼ oz snipped fresh chives, to garnish

1 Heat the butter in a large saucepan over a medium heat. Add the onions and cook, stirring frequently, for 5–8 minutes, or until soft. Add the potato and stir, then add the stock and bring to the boil. Reduce the heat and simmer for 5 minutes.

2 Add the broccoli and cook, stirring occasionally, for a further 5 minutes. Season to taste with pepper. Transfer the soup to a food processor or blender, in batches, and process until smooth. Return to a clean saucepan.

3 Add 150 ml/5 fl oz of the cream and 150 g/5½ oz of the cheese to the soup and cook over a low heat, stirring, until the cheese has melted.

4 Mash the remaining cheese with the remaining cream in a bowl and pile some onto each of the toast slices.

5 Serve the soup hot in individual warmed bowls, topped with the cheesy toast slices and sprinkled with a few chives.

Leek & Potato Soup

Serves 4–6

ingredients
- 55 g/2 oz butter
- 1 onion, chopped
- 3 leeks, sliced
- 225 g/8 oz potatoes, peeled and cut into 2-cm/¾-inch cubes
- 850 ml/1½ pints vegetable stock
- salt and pepper
- 150 ml/5 fl oz single cream (optional) and 2 tbsp snipped fresh chives, to garnish

1 Melt the butter in a large saucepan over a medium heat, add the vegetables and sauté gently for 2–3 minutes, until soft but not brown. Pour in the stock, bring to the boil, then reduce the heat and simmer, covered, for 15 minutes.

2 Remove from the heat and liquidize the soup in the saucepan using a hand-held blender if you have one. Otherwise, pour into a blender, liquidize until smooth and return to the rinsed-out saucepan.

3 Heat the soup, season to taste with salt and pepper and serve in warmed bowls, swirled with the cream, if using, and garnished with chives.

Scotch Broth

Serves 6–8

ingredients
- 700 g/1 lb 9 oz neck of lamb
- 1.7 litres/3 pints water
- 55 g/2 oz pearl barley
- 2 onions, chopped
- 1 garlic clove, finely chopped
- 3 small turnips, cut into small dice
- 3 carrots, peeled and finely sliced
- 2 celery sticks, sliced
- 2 leeks, sliced
- salt and pepper
- 2 tbsp chopped fresh parsley, to garnish

1 Cut the meat into small pieces, removing as much fat as possible. Put into a large saucepan and cover with the water. Bring to the boil over a medium heat and skim off any scum that appears.

2 Add the pearl barley, reduce the heat and cook gently, covered, for 1 hour.

3 Add the vegetables and season well with salt and pepper. Continue to cook for a further hour. Remove from the heat and leave to cool slightly.

4 Remove the meat from the pan using a slotted spoon and strip the meat from the bones. Discard the bones and any fat or gristle. Place the meat back in the pan and leave to cool thoroughly, then refrigerate overnight.

5 Scrape the solidified fat off the surface of the soup. Reheat, season to taste with salt and pepper and serve piping hot, with the parsley scattered over the top.

Cullen Skink

Serves 4

ingredients
- 225 g/8 oz undyed smoked haddock fillet
- 2 tbsp butter
- 1 onion, finely chopped
- 600 ml/1 pint milk
- 350 g/12 oz potatoes, diced
- 350 g/12 oz cod, boned, skinned and cubed
- 150 ml/5 fl oz double cream
- 2 tbsp chopped fresh parsley
- lemon juice, to taste (optional)
- salt and pepper
- lemon slices and fresh parsley sprigs, to garnish

1 Put the haddock fillet in a large frying pan and cover with boiling water. Leave to stand for 10 minutes. Drain, reserving 300 ml/10 fl oz of the soaking water. Flake the fish, taking care to remove all the bones.

2 Heat the butter in a large saucepan over a low heat. Add the onion and cook for 10 minutes, or until soft. Add the milk and bring to a gentle simmer before adding the potatoes. Cook for 10 minutes.

3 Add the reserved haddock and cod. Simmer for a further 10 minutes, or until the cod is tender.

4 Remove about one third of the fish and potatoes, transfer to a food processor and blend until smooth. Alternatively, push through a sieve into a bowl. Return to the saucepan with the cream and parsley, and salt and pepper to taste. Add lemon juice, if using. Add a little of the reserved soaking water if the soup seems too thick. Reheat gently and serve, garnished with lemon slices and parsley sprigs.

Classic Sandwich Selection

Serves 4

ingredients
- 8 slices thinly sliced white, brown or wholemeal bread
- 55 g/2 oz butter, softened
- salt and pepper

egg & cress
- 4 hard-boiled free-range eggs, shelled and chopped
- 2 tbsp mayonnaise
- ½ punnet fresh cress

cucumber
- ½ cucumber, finely sliced

roast beef & horseradish
- 115 g/4 oz sliced rare roast beef
- 2 tbsp creamed horseradish

smoked salmon & cream cheese
- 115 g/4 oz cream cheese
- 4 slices smoked salmon
- juice of 1 lemon

1 Cut off the bread crusts with a serrated knife and butter each slice.

2 For the Egg & Cress sandwiches mix the egg with the mayonnaise. Cut the cress from the punnet with a pair of scissors and stir into the mixture. Divide the mixture between 4 slices of bread, season to taste and top with the remaining slices. Press down firmly and then cut into four squares or triangles or three fingers.

3 For the Cucumber sandwiches arrange the cucumber on 4 slices of bread and season with lots of pepper. Top with the remaining bread slices and cut to shape.

4 For the Roast Beef & Horseradish sandwiches arrange the beef on 4 slices of bread and spread the other slices with the horseradish sauce. Layer them together and cut into shapes.

5 For the Smoked Salmon & Cream Cheese sandwiches spread the cheese on 4 slices of bread (you can omit the butter from these slices) and arrange the smoked salmon on top. Sprinkle with lemon juice and season with pepper. Form the sandwiches and cut into shapes.

6 Serve the sandwiches immediately.

Ploughman's with Chutney

Serves 4

ingredients
- 4 large eggs
- 225 g/8 oz British cheese, such as farmhouse, Cheddar cheese, Stilton and/or Somerset brie
- 300 g/10½ oz ready-made pork pie
- 1 carrot
- 8 spring onions
- 16 baby vine tomatoes
- 4 slices cured ham
- 4 tbsp chutney of your choice
- 85 g/3 oz salad leaves
- crusty bread, to serve

1 Bring a small saucepan of water to the boil. Gently lower the eggs into the water using a long-handled spoon. Keep the water at a gentle simmer and cook for 4–5 minutes, or until cooked to your liking. Remove the eggs using a slotted spoon and drain quickly on kitchen paper. Leave to cool.

2 When the eggs are cool enough to handle, remove and discard the shells. Cut the eggs in half. Cut the cheese into wedges and the pork pie into quarters. Peel the carrots and cut into batons.

3 Arrange equal portions of each of the ingredients on individual serving plates. Serve immediately with crusty bread.

Welsh Rarebit

Serves 4

ingredients
- 4 thick slices white bread or brown bread
- 225 g/8 oz mature Cheddar cheese, grated
- 25 g/1 oz butter
- 3 tbsp beer
- ½ tsp mustard powder
- 1 egg, beaten
- salt and pepper

1 Toast the bread under a medium grill on one side only.

2 Put the cheese into a saucepan and add the butter and beer. Heat slowly over a low heat, stirring continuously. Add some salt and pepper and the mustard powder and stir well until the mixture is thick and creamy. Remove from the heat and leave to cool slightly before mixing in the egg.

3 Spread the rarebit generously over the untoasted side of the bread and place under a hot grill until golden and bubbling. Serve immediately.

Pan Haggerty

Serves 4–5

ingredients
- 4 tbsp olive oil
- 55 g/2 oz butter
- 450 g/1 lb firm potatoes, such as Desirée or waxy salad potatoes
- 225 g/8 oz onions, halved and thinly sliced
- 115 g/4 oz Cheddar cheese, grated
- salt and pepper

1 Heat half the olive oil and half the butter in a 23-cm/9-inch frying pan.

2 Peel the potatoes if necessary (you don't need to peel small salad potatoes). Slice thinly using a mandolin or food processor. Rinse the slices quickly in cold water and dry thoroughly using a tea towel or kitchen paper.

3 Remove the oil and butter from the heat and arrange the sliced potato in the base of the pan. Build up layers of potato, onion and cheese, seasoning well with salt and pepper between each layer. Finish with a layer of potato and dot the remaining butter over the top.

4 Return to the heat and cook over a medium heat for 15–20 minutes. The base should become brown but not burn. Place a large plate over the pan and invert the potato onto the plate by tilting the pan. Add the remaining oil to the pan and slip the potato back in, cooking the other side for a further 15 minutes until the base is crusty.

5 Remove from the heat and serve immediately on warmed plates.

Ham & Egg Pie

Serves 4

ingredients
- 4 eggs
- 175 g/6 oz cooked ham
- 3 spring onions, finely chopped
- 150 ml/5 fl oz milk
- salt and pepper

pastry
- 250 g/9 oz plain flour
- 115g/4 oz butter
- pinch of salt
- 2–3 tbs cold water to mix

1 Preheat the oven to 200°C/400°F/ Gas Mark 6.

2 To make the pastry, put the flour into a bowl, rub in the butter until the mixture resembles fine breadcrumbs, then season and add enough water to make a smooth dough.

3 Bring a small saucepan of water to the boil, add 2 eggs and cook for 8 minutes, then cool quickly in cold water.

4 Divide the pastry in two, one piece slightly larger than the other, and roll out the larger piece to line a 20-cm/8-inch flan tin.

5 Peel and chop the hard-boiled eggs and cut the ham into small pieces. Place the eggs, ham and onions in the pastry case.

6 Beat the remaining eggs with the milk, season well with salt and pepper and pour over the ham mixture.

7 Roll out the other piece of pastry, dampen the edge of the pastry base and lay the lid on top. Seal well and crimp the edges of the pie. Glaze with a little milk and place the pie on a baking sheet.

8 Bake in the preheated oven for 10 minutes then reduce the oven temperature to 180°C/350°F/Gas Mark 4 and bake for a further 30 minutes, until the pastry is golden. Serve warm or cold.

Cornish Pasties

Serves 4

ingredients

- 250 g/9 oz chuck steak, trimmed and cut into 1-cm/½-inch dice
- 175 g/6 oz swede, peeled and cut into 1-cm/½-inch dice
- 350 g/12 oz potatoes, peeled and cut into 1-cm/½-inch dice
- 1 onion, finely chopped
- 1 egg, beaten
- butter, for greasing
- salt and pepper

pastry

- 450 g/1 lb plain flour, plus extra for dusting
- pinch of salt
- 115 g/4 oz lard
- 115 g/4 oz butter
- 175 ml/6 fl oz cold water

1 To make the pastry, sift the flour and salt into a bowl and gently rub in the lard and butter until the mixture resembles breadcrumbs. Add the water, a spoonful at a time, and stir the mixture with a knife until it holds together.

2 Turn out onto a lightly floured surface and gently press together until smooth. Wrap in clingfilm and leave to chill for 1 hour.

3 Meanwhile, to prepare the filling, mix the meat and vegetables together and season well with salt and pepper.

4 Divide the pastry into four even-sized pieces and roll one out until just larger than the size of a 20-cm/8-inch plate. Place the plate on top of the pastry and cut round it to give a neat edge. Repeat with the other pieces.

5 Arrange the meat and vegetable mixture across the four rounds of pastry, making sure the filling goes almost to the edge.

6 Brush the edges of the pastry with water, then bring the edges up over the filling and press together to form a ridge. You can flute the edges of the pasties with your fingers or fold over the pastry to form a cord-like seal. Tuck in the ends. Leave to chill for 1 hour, then glaze with the egg.

7 Meanwhile, preheat the oven to 190°C/375°F/Gas Mark 5 and grease a baking tray.

8 Place the pasties on the baking tray and cook in the centre of the preheated oven for 50–60 minutes. The pasties should be crisp and golden in colour. If the pastry is getting too brown, cover with foil and reduce the oven temperature. Serve warm.

Pork & Apple Pie

Serves 8

ingredients
- 900 g/2 lb waxy potatoes, peeled and sliced
- 2 tbsp butter
- 2 tbsp vegetable oil
- 450 g/1 lb lean boneless pork, cubed
- 2 onions, sliced
- 4 garlic cloves, crushed
- 600 ml/1 pint stock
- 2 tbsp chopped fresh sage
- 2 eating apples, peeled, cored and sliced
- 1 egg, beaten
- 1 tsp gelatine
- salt and pepper

pastry
- 675 g/1 lb 8 oz plain flour, plus extra for dusting
- pinch of salt
- 4 tbsp butter
- 125 g/4½ oz lard
- 300 ml/10 fl oz water

1 Bring a large saucepan of lightly salted water to the boil, add the potatoes and cook for 10 minutes. Drain and set aside. Melt the butter with the oil in a flameproof casserole over a medium–high heat. Add the pork and cook until browned all over.

2 Add the onions and garlic and cook, stirring frequently, for 5 minutes. Stir in the pork, stock and sage. Season to taste with salt and pepper. Reduce the heat, cover and simmer for 1½ hours. Drain the stock from the casserole and reserve. Leave the pork to cool.

3 Preheat the oven to 200°C/400°F/ Gas Mark 6. To make the pastry, sift the flour and salt into a bowl. Make a well in the centre. Melt the butter and lard in a saucepan with the water, then bring to the boil. Pour into the well and gradually mix into the flour to form a dough. Turn out onto a lightly floured surface and knead until smooth.

4 Reserve a quarter of the dough and use the remainder to line the base and sides of a large pie tin or deep 20-cm/8-inch round loose-based cake tin. Alternatively, use the dough to line eight individual tart tins.

5 Layer the pork, potatoes and apples in the base of the tin or tins. Roll out the reserved pastry to make a lid. Dampen the edges and put the lid on top, sealing well. Brush with the beaten egg to glaze. Make a hole in the top. Bake in the preheated oven for 30 minutes, then reduce the temperature to 160°C/325°F/ Gas Mark 3 and bake for a further 45 minutes. Dissolve the gelatine in the reserved stock and pour into the hole in the lid as the pie cools. Serve well chilled.

Chapter 3
Classic Pub Grub

Prawn Cocktail

Serves 4

ingredients
- ½ Webbs lettuce, finely shredded
- 150 ml/5 fl oz mayonnaise
- 2 tbsp single cream
- 2 tbsp tomato ketchup
- few drops of Tabasco sauce, or to taste
- juice of ½ lemon, or to taste
- 175 g/6 oz cooked peeled prawns
- salt and pepper
- thinly sliced buttered brown bread, to serve (optional)

to garnish
- paprika, for sprinkling
- 4 cooked prawns, in their shells
- 4 lemon slices

1 Divide the lettuce between four small serving dishes (traditionally, stemmed glass ones are used, but any small dishes will be fine).

2 Mix the mayonnaise, cream and tomato ketchup together in a bowl. Add the Tabasco sauce and lemon juice and season well with salt and pepper.

3 Divide the prawns equally between the dishes and pour over the dressing. Cover and leave to chill in the refrigerator for 30 minutes.

4 Sprinkle a little paprika over the cocktails and garnish each dish with a prawn and a lemon slice. Serve the cocktails with the brown bread, if using.

Coronation Chicken

Serves 6

ingredients
- 4 boneless chicken breasts
- 1 bay leaf
- 1 small onion, sliced
- 1 carrot, sliced
- 4 peppercorns
- 1 tbsp olive oil
- 2 shallots, finely chopped
- 2 tsp mild curry paste
- 2 tsp tomato purée
- juice of ½ lemon
- 300 ml/10 fl oz mayonnaise
- 150 ml/5 fl oz natural yogurt
- 85 g/3 oz ready-to-eat dried apricots, chopped
- salt and pepper
- 2 tbsp chopped fresh parsley, to garnish

1 Place the chicken breasts in a large saucepan with the bay leaf, onion and carrot. Cover with water and add ½ teaspoon salt and the peppercorns. Bring to the boil over a medium heat, reduce the heat and simmer very gently for 20–25 minutes. Remove from the heat and allow to cool in the liquor. Drain off 150 ml/5 fl oz of the stock for the sauce.

2 Meanwhile, heat the oil in a frying pan, add the shallots and sauté gently for 2–3 minutes until soft but not coloured. Stir in the curry paste and continue to cook for a further minute. Stir in the reserved stock, the tomato purée and the lemon juice and simmer for 10 minutes until the sauce is quite thick. Leave to cool.

3 Remove the chicken from the stock, take off the skin and slice the meat into neat pieces.

4 Mix together the mayonnaise and the yogurt and stir into the sauce. Add the chopped apricots and season to taste with salt and pepper.

5 Stir the chicken into the sauce until well coated and turn into a serving dish. Leave to stand for at least 1 hour to allow the flavours to mingle. Serve garnished with the chopped parsley.

Beef Stew with Herb Dumplings

Serves 6

ingredients

- 3 tbsp olive oil
- 2 onions, finely sliced
- 2 garlic cloves, chopped
- 1 kg/2 lb 4 oz good-quality braising steak
- 2 tbsp plain flour
- 300 ml/10 fl oz beef stock
- bouquet garni
- 150 ml/5 fl oz red wine
- salt and pepper
- 1 tbsp chopped fresh parsley, to garnish

herb dumplings

- 115 g/4 oz self-raising flour, plus extra for shaping
- 55 g/2 oz suet or vegetable shortening
- 1 tsp mustard
- 1 tbsp chopped fresh parsley
- 1 tsp chopped fresh sage
- 4 tbsp cold water
- salt and pepper

1 Preheat the oven to 150°C/300°F/ Gas Mark 2.

2 Heat 1 tablespoon of the oil in a large frying pan, then add the onion and garlic and fry until soft and brown. Remove from the pan using a slotted spoon and place in a large casserole dish.

3 Trim the meat and cut into thick strips. Add the remaining oil to the pan, then add the meat and fry over a high heat, stirring well, until brown all over.

4 Sprinkle in the flour and stir well to prevent lumps forming. Season well with salt and pepper.

5 Over a medium heat, pour in the stock, stirring all the time to make a smooth sauce, then continue to heat until boiling.

6 Carefully turn the contents of the pan into the casserole dish. Add the bouquet garni and the wine. Cover and cook gently for 2–2½ hours.

7 Start making the dumplings 20 minutes before the stew is ready. Place the flour, suet, mustard, parsley, sage and salt and pepper to taste in a bowl and mix well. Add enough of the water to the mixture to form a firm but soft dough. Break the dough into 12 pieces and roll them into round dumplings (you might need some flour on your hands for this).

8 Remove the stew from the oven, check the seasoning, discard the bouquet garni and add the dumplings, pushing them down under the liquid. Cover and return the dish to the oven for 15 minutes, or until the dumplings have doubled in size.

9 Serve piping hot with the parsley scattered over the top.

Yorkshire Puddings

Serves 4

ingredients
- 100 g/3½ oz plain flour
- 1 egg, beaten
- 300 ml/10 fl oz milk and water mixed (half milk, half water)
- 3 tbsp roast beef dripping, goose fat or olive oil
- salt and pepper

1 Preheat the oven to 220ºC/425ºF/ Gas Mark 7. Place the flour and a pinch of salt in a mixing bowl. Make a well in the centre, then add the egg and half the liquid. Using a whisk, beat the egg and milk and water mixture together and gradually incorporate the flour. Continue beating until the mixture is smooth and there are no lumps. Gradually beat in the remaining liquid. Season to taste with pepper.

2 Put a little dripping into each mould of a 12-hole bun tin. Heat at the top of the preheated oven for 3–4 minutes until very hot. Remove the hot tray very carefully, use a ladle to pour some batter into each mould, then return the tray to the oven.

3 Bake for 20–25 minutes until the Yorkshire puddings are well puffed up and golden brown. Serve immediately with roast beef or any other meat you wish.

Steak & Kidney Pie

Serves 4–6

ingredients

- butter, for greasing
- 700 g/1 lb 9 oz braising steak, trimmed and cut into 4-cm/1½-inch pieces
- 3 lambs' kidneys, cored and cut into 2.5-cm/1-inch pieces
- 2 tbsp plain flour
- 3 tbsp vegetable oil
- 1 onion, roughly chopped
- 1 garlic clove, finely chopped
- 125 ml/4 fl oz red wine
- 450 ml/16 fl oz stock
- 1 bay leaf
- 400 g/14 oz ready-made puff pastry
- 1 egg, beaten
- salt and pepper

1 Preheat the oven to 160°C/325°F/ Gas Mark 3. Grease a 1.2-litre/2-pint pie dish.

2 Put the prepared meat with the flour and salt and pepper in a large polythene bag and shake well until all the meat is well coated.

3 Heat the oil in a flameproof casserole over a high heat, add the meat in batches and brown. Remove from the casserole with a slotted spoon and keep warm. Add the onion and garlic to the casserole and fry for 2–3 minutes until beginning to soften.

4 Stir in the wine and scrape the base of the pan to release the sediment. Pour in the stock, stirring constantly, and bring to the boil. Leave to bubble for 2–3 minutes. Add the bay leaf and return the meat to the casserole. Cover and cook in the centre of the oven for 1½–2 hours. Check the seasoning, then remove the bay leaf. Leave the meat to cool, preferably overnight, to develop the flavours.

5 Preheat the oven to 200°C/400°F/ Gas Mark 6.

6 Roll out the pastry on a lightly floured work surface to about 7 cm/2¾ inches larger than the pie dish. Cut off a 3-cm/ 1¼-inch strip from the edge of the pastry. Moisten the rim of the dish and press the pastry strip onto it. Place a pie funnel in the centre of the dish and spoon in the steak and kidney filling. Do not overfill, keeping any extra gravy to serve separately. Moisten the pastry collar with water and put on the pastry lid, fitting it carefully around the pie funnel. Crimp the edges of the pastry firmly and glaze with the egg.

7 Place the pie on a tray towards the top of the preheated oven for about 30 minutes. The pie should be golden brown and the filling bubbling hot; cover it with foil and reduce the temperature if the pastry is getting too brown.

Irish Stew

Serves 4

ingredients
- 4 tbsp plain flour
- 1.3 kg/3 lb middle neck of lamb, trimmed of visible fat
- 3 large onions, chopped
- 3 carrots, sliced
- 450 g/1 lb potatoes, quartered
- ½ tsp dried thyme
- 850 ml/1½ pints hot beef stock
- salt and pepper
- 2 tbsp chopped fresh parsley, to garnish

1 Preheat the oven to 160°C/325°F/ Gas Mark 3. Spread the flour on a plate and season with salt and pepper. Roll the pieces of lamb in the flour to coat, shaking off any excess, and arrange in the base of a casserole.

2 Layer the onions, carrots and potatoes on top of the lamb.

3 Sprinkle in the thyme and pour in the stock, then cover and cook in the preheated oven for 2½ hours. Garnish with the chopped fresh parsley and serve straight from the casserole.

Pork Hot Pot

Serves 6

ingredients

- 85 g/3 oz plain flour
- 1.3 kg/3 lb pork fillet, cut into 5-mm/¼-inch slices
- 4 tbsp sunflower oil
- 2 onions, thinly sliced
- 2 garlic cloves
- 400 g/14 oz canned chopped tomatoes
- 350 ml/12 fl oz dry white wine
- 1 tbsp torn fresh basil leaves
- 2 tbsp chopped fresh parsley
- salt and pepper
- fresh oregano, to garnish
- fresh crusty bread, to serve

1 Spread the flour on a plate and season with salt and pepper. Coat the pork slices in the flour, shaking off any excess.

2 Heat the oil in a flameproof casserole. Add the pork slices and cook over a medium heat, turning occasionally, for 4–5 minutes, or until browned all over. Transfer to a plate with a slotted spoon and reserve.

3 Add the onion slices to the casserole and cook over a low heat, stirring occasionally, for 10 minutes, or until golden brown.

4 Finely chop the garlic, add to the casserole and cook for a further 2 minutes, then add the tomatoes, wine and basil and season to taste with salt and pepper. Cook, stirring frequently, for 3 minutes.

5 Return the pork to the casserole, cover and simmer gently for 1 hour, or until the meat is tender. Scatter over the parsley, garnish with oregano and serve with fresh crusty bread.

Braised Lamb Shanks

Serves 6

ingredients
- 1 tsp coriander seeds
- 1 tsp cumin seeds
- 1 tsp ground cinnamon
- 1 fresh green chilli, deseeded and finely chopped
- 1 garlic bulb, separated into cloves
- 125 ml/4 fl oz groundnut oil or sunflower oil
- grated rind of 1 lime
- 6 lamb shanks
- 2 onions, chopped
- 2 carrots, chopped
- 2 celery sticks, chopped
- 1 lime, chopped
- about 700 ml/1¼ pints beef stock or water
- 1 tsp sun-dried tomato purée
- 2 fresh mint sprigs
- 2 fresh rosemary sprigs, plus extra to garnish
- salt and pepper

1 Dry-fry the coriander seeds and cumin seeds until fragrant, then pound with the cinnamon, chilli and 2 garlic cloves with a mortar and pestle. Stir in half the oil and the lime rind. Rub the spice paste all over the lamb and marinate for 4 hours.

2 Preheat the oven to 200°C/400°F/ Gas Mark 6. Heat the remaining oil in a flameproof casserole and cook the lamb, turning frequently, until evenly browned. Chop the remaining garlic and add to the casserole with the onions, carrots, celery and lime, then pour in enough stock or water to cover. Stir in the tomato purée, add the herbs and season to taste with salt and pepper.

3 Cover and cook in the preheated oven for 30 minutes. Reduce the oven temperature to 160°C/325°F/ Gas Mark 3 and cook for a further 3 hours, or until the lamb is very tender.

4 Transfer the lamb to a warmed dish. Strain the cooking liquid to remove any solids, then return the liquid to the casserole. Boil until reduced and thickened. Serve the lamb with the sauce poured over it, garnished with sprigs of fresh rosemary.

Gammon Steaks with Fried Egg & Chips

Serves 4

ingredients

- vegetable oil, for frying and brushing
- 6 large potatoes, Desirée or Maris Piper, peeled and cut into even-sized chips
- 4 x 175 g/6 oz gammon steaks
- 4 eggs

1 Heat the oil in a deep-fat fryer or a large saucepan to 120°C/250°F. Add the chips and fry for about 8–10 minutes until soft but not coloured. Remove from the oil and increase the temperature to 180–190°C/350–375°F.

2 Meanwhile place the gammon steaks on a grill pan and brush with a little oil. Grill for 3-4 minutes on either side, turning occasionally until the fat is crisp. Set aside and keep warm.

3 Return the chips to the fryer at the increased temperature and cook for a further 2–3 minutes until they are golden brown and crisp. Drain, season well and keep warm.

4 Put 2 tablespoons of oil into a frying pan and heat over a medium heat. Break two eggs into the pan and cook for a few seconds until the white is setting. Tip the pan and spoon the hot oil over the egg yolks so that they become firm but still soft. Remove the eggs from the pan using a wooden spatula and drain on kitchen paper. Keep warm and repeat with the other eggs.

5 Arrange the ham, egg and chips on warmed plates and serve immediately.

Sausage & Mash with Onion Gravy

Serves 4

ingredients
- 8 good-quality sausages
- 1 tbsp oil

onion gravy
- 3 onions, halved and thinly sliced
- 70 g/2½ oz butter
- 125 ml/4 fl oz Marsala or port
- 125 ml/4 fl oz vegetable stock
- salt and pepper

mash
- 900 g/2 lb floury potatoes, such as King Edward, Maris Piper or Desirée, peeled and cut into chunks
- 55 g/2 oz butter
- 3 tbsp hot milk
- 2 tbsp chopped fresh parsley
- salt and pepper

1 Put the sausages in a frying pan with the oil and cook slowly over a low heat for 25–30 minutes. Cover the pan and turn the sausages from time to time. Don't rush the cooking, because you want them well-cooked and sticky.

2 Meanwhile, prepare the onion gravy. Add the onions to a frying pan with the butter and fry over a low heat, stirring constantly, until soft. Continue to cook for about 30 minutes, until the onions are brown and almost melting, stirring from time to time.

3 Pour in the Marsala and stock and continue to bubble away until the onion gravy is really thick. Season to taste with salt and pepper.

4 To make the mash, bring a large saucepan of lightly salted water to the boil. Add the potatoes and cook for 15–20 minutes. Drain well and mash with a potato masher until smooth. Season with salt and pepper, add the butter, milk and parsley and stir well.

5 Serve the sausages really hot with the mash. Spoon a generous serving of the onion gravy over the top.

Fisherman's Pie

Serves 6

ingredients
- 900 g/2 lb white fish fillets, such as plaice, skinned
- 150 ml/5 fl oz dry white wine
- 1 tbsp chopped fresh parsley, tarragon or dill
- 175 g/6 oz small mushrooms, sliced
- 100 g/3½ oz butter, plus extra for greasing
- 175 g/6 oz cooked, peeled prawns
- 40 g/1½ oz plain flour
- 125 ml/4 fl oz double cream
- 900 g/2 lb floury potatoes, such as King Edward, Maris Piper or Desirée, peeled and cut into chunks
- salt and pepper

1 Preheat the oven to 180°C/350°F/Gas Mark 4. Grease a 1.7-litre/3-pint baking dish.

2 Fold the fish fillets in half and place in the dish. Season well with salt and pepper, pour over the wine and scatter over the herbs. Cover with foil and bake for 15 minutes until the fish starts to flake. Strain off the liquid and reserve for the sauce. Increase the oven temperature to 220°C/425°F/Gas Mark 7.

3 Add the mushrooms to a frying pan with 15 g/½ oz of the butter and sauté. Spoon the mushrooms over the fish and scatter over the prawns.

4 Add 55 g/2 oz of the butter to a saucepan, heat and stir in the flour. Cook for a few minutes without browning, remove from the heat, then add the reserved cooking liquid gradually, stirring well between each addition.

5 Return to the heat and gently bring to the boil, still stirring to ensure a smooth sauce. Add the cream and season to taste with salt and pepper. Pour over the fish in the dish and smooth over the surface.

6 Make the mashed potato by cooking the potatoes in boiling salted water for 15–20 minutes. Drain well and mash with a potato masher until smooth. Season to taste with salt and pepper and add the remaining butter, stirring until melted.

7 Pile or pipe the potato onto the fish and sauce and bake in the oven for 10–15 minutes until golden brown.

Vegetable Toad-In-The-Hole

Serves 4

ingredients
- 25 g/1 oz butter
- 2 garlic cloves, crushed
- 1 onion, cut into eighths
- 75 g/2¾ oz baby carrots, halved lengthways
- 50 g/1¾ oz French beans
- 50 g/1¾ oz canned sweetcorn, drained
- 2 tomatoes, deseeded and cut into chunks
- 1 tsp wholegrain mustard
- 1 tbsp chopped fresh mixed herbs

salt and pepper

batter
- 100 g/3½ oz plain flour
- 2 eggs, beaten
- 200 ml/7 fl oz milk
- 2 tbsp wholegrain mustard
- 2 tbsp vegetable oil
- salt

1 To make the batter, sift the flour and a pinch of salt into a bowl. Beat in the eggs and milk to make a batter. Stir in the mustard and leave to stand.

2 Meanwhile, preheat the oven to 200°C/400°F/Gas Mark 6. Pour the oil into a shallow ovenproof dish and heat in the preheated oven for 10 minutes.

3 Melt the butter in a frying pan, add the garlic and onion and sauté, stirring constantly, for 2 minutes. Bring a saucepan of lightly salted water to the boil, add the carrots and beans and cook for 7 minutes, or until tender. Drain well.

4 Add the sweetcorn and tomatoes to the frying pan with the mustard and herbs. Season well with salt and pepper and add the carrots and beans.

5 Remove the heated dish from the oven and pour in the batter. Spoon the vegetables into the centre, return to the oven and cook for 30–35 minutes, until the batter has risen and set. Serve immediately on warmed plates.

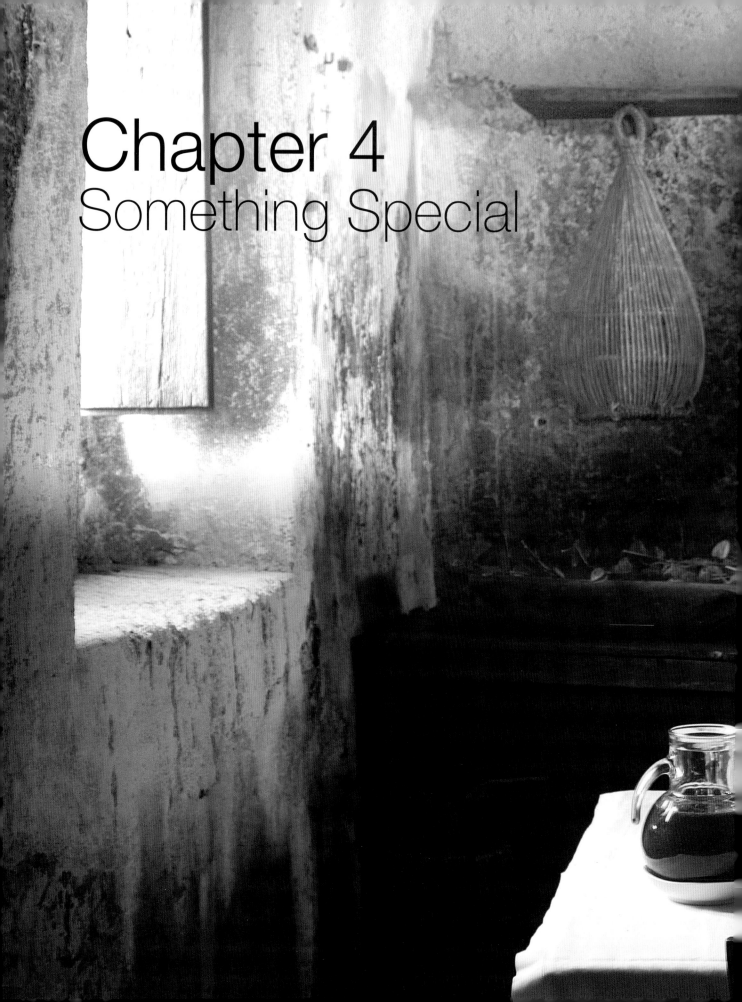

Chapter 4
Something Special

Beef Wellington

Serves 6

ingredients

- 2 tbsp olive oil or vegetable oil
- 1.5 kg/3 lb 5 oz beef fillet, cut from the middle of the fillet, trimmed of fat and sinew
- 55 g/2 oz butter
- 150 g/5 oz mushrooms, chopped
- 2 garlic cloves, crushed
- 150 g/5 oz smooth liver pâté
- few drops of truffle oil (optional)
- 1 tbsp fresh parsley, finely chopped
- 2 tsp English mustard
- 500 g/1 lb 2 oz ready-made puff pastry
- 1 egg, lightly beaten
- salt and pepper
- wilted greens and roasted root vegetables, including parsnips, to serve

1 Place a large frying pan over a high heat and add the olive oil. Rub salt and pepper into the beef, place it in the pan and sear very quickly all over. (This method gives a rare version. If you want it less rare, roast it at 220°C/425°F/Gas Mark 7, for 20 minutes at this stage.) Set aside to cool.

2 Heat the butter in a frying pan over a medium heat, add the mushrooms and fry for 5 minutes. Reduce the heat, add the garlic and fry for a further 5 minutes. Put the mushrooms and garlic in a bowl, add the pâté, truffle oil, if using, and parsley, and mash with a fork. Leave to cool.

3 Rub the mustard into the seared beef fillet. Roll out the pastry into a rectangle large enough to wrap the whole fillet with some to spare. Spread the mushroom paste in the middle of the pastry in a shape the size of the base of the beef and lay the beef on top. Brush the edges of the pastry with beaten egg and fold it over, edges overlapping, and across the meat to completely enclose it.

4 Preheat the oven to 200°C/425°F/Gas Mark 7. Place the wrapped beef in a roasting tin with the join underneath and brush with beaten egg. Leave to chill in the refrigerator for 15 minutes, then transfer to the preheated oven and bake for 50 minutes. Check after 30 minutes – if the pastry looks golden brown, cover it with foil to prevent it burning.

5 Carve the beef into thick slices and serve on warmed plates with wilted greens and roasted root vegetables.

Roast Gammon

Serves 6

ingredients

- 1.3 kg/3 lb boneless gammon, pre-soaked if necessary
- 2 tbsp Dijon mustard
- 85 g/3 oz demerara sugar
- ½ tsp ground cinnamon
- ½ tsp ground ginger
- 18 whole cloves
- Cumberland sauce, to serve

1 Place the joint in a large saucepan, cover with cold water and slowly bring to the boil over a gentle heat. Cover and simmer very gently for 1 hour.

2 Preheat the oven to 200°C/400°F/ Gas Mark 6.

3 Remove the gammon from the pan and drain. Remove the rind and discard. Score the fat into a diamond-shaped pattern with a sharp knife.

4 Spread the mustard over the fat. Mix together the sugar and the spices on a plate and roll the gammon in it, pressing down well to coat evenly.

5 Stud the diamond shapes with cloves and place the joint in a roasting tin. Roast for 20 minutes until the glaze is a rich golden colour.

6 To serve hot, leave to stand for 20 minutes before carving. If the gammon is to be served cold, it can be cooked a day ahead. Serve with Cumberland sauce.

Game Pie

Serves 4–6

ingredients

- oil, for greasing
- 700 g/1 lb 9 oz mixed game, cut into 3-cm/1¼-inch pieces
- 2 tbsp plain flour, plus extra for dusting
- 3 tbsp vegetable oil
- 1 onion, roughly chopped
- 1 garlic clove, finely chopped
- 350 g/12 oz large field mushrooms, sliced
- 1 tsp crushed juniper berries
- 125 ml/4 fl oz port or Marsala
- 450 ml/16 fl oz chicken stock or game stock
- 1 bay leaf
- 400 g/14 oz ready-made puff pastry
- 1 egg, beaten
- salt and pepper

1 Preheat the oven to 160°C/325°F/ Gas Mark 3. Grease a 1.2-litre/2-pint pie dish. Put the meat into a large polythene bag with the flour and salt and pepper and shake to coat the meat.

2 Heat the oil in a large flameproof casserole dish over a high heat and brown the meat in batches. Remove with a slotted spoon and keep warm. Fry the onion and garlic for 2–3 minutes until soft, then add the mushrooms and cook for 2 minutes, stirring constantly, until they start to wilt. Add the juniper berries, then the port and scrape the bits from the base of the casserole. Add the stock, stirring constantly, and bring to the boil. Leave to bubble for 2–3 minutes. Add the bay leaf and return the meat to the casserole.

3 Cover and cook in the preheated oven for 1½–2 hours until the meat is tender. Check for seasoning and add more salt and pepper if necessary. Remove from the oven and leave to cool. Chill overnight to develop the flavours. Remove the bay leaf.

4 Preheat the oven to 200°C/400°F/ Gas Mark 6.

5 Roll out the pastry on a lightly floured work surface to about 7 cm/2¾ inches larger than the pie dish. Cut off a 3-cm/ 1¼-inch strip around the edge. Moisten the rim of the dish and press the pastry strip onto it. Place a pie funnel in the centre of the dish and spoon in the meat filling. Do not overfill, keeping any extra gravy to serve separately.

6 Moisten the pastry collar with a little water and put on the pastry lid. Crimp the edges of the pastry firmly and glaze with the egg.

7 Bake the pie on a tray near the top of the preheated oven for about 30 minutes. If necessary, cover it with foil and reduce the oven temperature a little. The pie should be golden brown and the filling bubbling hot. Serve hot, on warmed plates.

Venison Casserole

Serves 4–6

ingredients

- 3 tbsp olive oil
- 1 kg/2 lb 4 oz casserole venison, cut into 3-cm/1¼-inch cubes
- 2 onions, finely sliced
- 2 garlic cloves, chopped
- 2 tbsp plain flour
- 350 ml/12 fl oz beef stock or vegetable stock
- 125 ml/4 fl oz port or red wine
- 2 tbsp redcurrant jelly
- 6 crushed juniper berries
- pinch of ground cinnamon
- whole nutmeg, for grating
- 175 g/6 oz vacuum-packed chestnuts (optional)
- salt and pepper

1 Preheat the oven to 150°C/300°F/ Gas Mark 2.

2 Heat the oil in a large frying pan, add the cubes of venison and brown over a high heat. You may need to fry the meat in two or three batches – do not overcrowd the pan. Remove the meat using a slotted spoon and place in a large casserole dish.

3 Add the onions and garlic to the pan and fry until golden, then add to the meat. Sprinkle the meat in the casserole dish with the flour and turn to coat evenly.

4 Gradually add the stock, scraping up the sediment at the base of the pan, then bring to the boil. Add to the casserole and stir, ensuring that the meat is covered.

5 Add the port, redcurrant jelly, juniper berries, cinnamon, a small grating of nutmeg and the chestnuts, if using. Season well with salt and pepper, then cover and cook gently in the centre of the preheated oven for 2–2½ hours.

6 Remove from the oven and season with more salt and pepper if necessary. Serve immediately, piping hot.

Roast Turkey with Two Stuffings

Serves 4–6

ingredients
- 4.5 kg/10 lb turkey
- 115 g/4 oz butter, softened
- 10 streaky bacon rashers
- salt and pepper
- Gravy, Cranberry Sauce and Bread Sauce (see page 104), to serve

celery & walnut
- 2 tbsp butter
- 2 onions, finely chopped
- 55 g/2 oz fresh wholemeal breadcrumbs
- 4 celery sticks, chopped
- 2 Cox's apples, cored and roughly chopped
- 115 g/4 oz dried ready-to-eat apricots, chopped
- 115 g/4 oz walnuts, chopped
- 2 tbsp chopped fresh parsley
- salt and pepper

chestnut
- 2 tbsp butter
- 115 g/4 oz lardons or strips of streaky bacon
- 1 onion, finely chopped
- 115 g/4 oz button mushrooms, sliced
- 225 g/8 oz chestnut purée
- 2 tbsp chopped fresh parsley
- grated rind of 2 lemons
- salt and pepper

1 To make the celery and walnut stuffing, put the butter in a frying pan, add the onions and cook until soft. In a bowl, mix together the breadcrumbs, celery, apples, apricots and walnuts. Add the cooked onion and season to taste with salt and pepper. Stir in the parsley. Leave to cool.

2 To make the chestnut stuffing, put the butter in a frying pan, add the lardons and onion and cook until soft. Add the mushrooms and cook for 1–2 minutes, then remove from the heat. In a bowl, mix together the chestnut purée with the parsley and lemon rind and season well with salt and pepper. Add the contents of the pan to the bowl and mix well. Leave to cool.

3 Preheat the oven to 220°C/425°F/ Gas Mark 7. Wipe the turkey inside and out with kitchen paper. Season, both inside and out, with salt and pepper.

4 Stuff the body cavity of the turkey with the Celery & Walnut stuffing and the neck with the Chestnut stuffing. Secure the neck skin with metal skewers and the legs with string.

5 Cover the bird all over with the butter and squeeze some under the breast skin. Use a little to grease the roasting tin. Place the bird in the tin, season again with salt and pepper and cover the breast with the bacon rashers. Cover with foil and roast in the oven for 30 minutes. Reduce the oven temperature to 180°C/350°F/ Gas Mark 4 and continue to cook for 2½–3 hours, basting the turkey every 30 minutes with the pan juices.

6 About 45 minutes before the end of the cooking time, remove the foil and allow the turkey to brown, basting from time to time. Remove the bacon rashers when crispy and keep warm.

7 Test that the turkey is cooked by piercing the thickest part of the leg with a sharp knife or skewer to make sure the juices run clear. Also, pull a leg slightly away from the body; it should feel loose.

8 Remove the turkey from the roasting tin and place on a warm serving plate, cover with foil and leave to rest whilst you complete the remainder of the meal. The turkey may be left to rest in this way for up to 1 hour before serving, accompanied by Gravy, Cranberry Sauce and Bread Sauce.

Accompaniments

Gravy

Remove the fat from the turkey roasting tin and place the tin over a low heat. Sprinkle in 1 tablespoon plain flour and stir well, using a small whisk to make a smooth paste. Cook for 1 minute. Gradually add 150 ml/5 fl oz hot chicken stock, whisking constantly, until smooth. Add 150 ml/5 fl oz red wine and leave to bubble until the gravy is slightly reduced. Season to taste with salt and pepper. Pour into a warmed jug and serve with the turkey.

Cranberry sauce

Place 225 g/8 oz fresh cranberries in a saucepan and add 85 g/3 oz soft brown sugar, 150 ml/5 fl oz orange juice, ½ teaspoon cinnamon and ½ teaspoon grated nutmeg. Bring to the boil slowly, stirring from time to time. Cook for about 8–10 minutes, or until the cranberries have burst, taking care as they may splash. Put the sauce in a serving bowl and cover until needed. Serve warm or cold with the turkey.

Bread sauce

Stud a peeled onion with 4 cloves, then place in a saucepan with 600 ml/1 pint milk, 115 g/4 oz fresh white breadcrumbs and 55 g/2 oz butter. Bring just to boiling point over a low heat, then remove from the heat and leave to stand in a warm place to infuse. Just before serving, remove the onion and gently reheat the sauce, beating well with a wooden spoon. Season to taste with salt and pepper and serve warm with the turkey.

Boned & Stuffed Roast Duck

Serves 6–8

ingredients

- 1.8 kg/4 lb duck (dressed weight), ask your butcher to bone the duck and cut off the wings at the first joint
- 450 g/1 lb flavoured sausage meat, such as pork and apricot
- 1 small onion, finely chopped
- 1 Cox's apple, cored and finely chopped
- 85 g/3 oz ready-to-eat dried apricots, finely chopped
- 85 g/3 oz chopped walnuts
- 2 tbsp chopped fresh parsley
- 1 large or 2 smaller duck breasts, skin removed
- salt and pepper

apricot sauce

- 400 g/14 oz canned apricot halves, in syrup
- 150 ml/5 fl oz chicken stock
- 125 ml/4 fl oz Marsala
- ½ tsp ground cinnamon
- ½ tsp ground ginger
- salt and pepper

1 Wipe the duck with kitchen paper both inside and out. Lay the bird skin-side down on a board and season well with salt and pepper.

2 Mix together the sausage meat, onion, apple, apricots, walnuts and parsley and season well with salt and pepper. Form into a large sausage shape.

3 Lay the duck breast(s) on the whole duck and cover with the stuffing. Wrap the whole duck around the filling and tuck in any leg and neck flaps.

4 Preheat the oven to 190°C/375°F/ Gas Mark 5. Sew the duck up the back and across both ends with fine string. Try to use one piece of string so that you can remove it in one go. Mould the duck into a good shape and place, sewn-side down, on a wire rack over a roasting tin.

5 Roast in the preheated oven for 1½–2 hours, basting occasionally. When it is cooked, the duck should be golden brown and crispy.

6 Meanwhile, make the apricot sauce. Put the apricots and their syrup into a blender and blend to a smooth purée. Pour into a saucepan, add the remaining ingredients and season to taste with salt and pepper. Stir over a low heat, then simmer for 2–3 minutes.

7 Keep the duck warm until ready to serve. Carve into thick slices and serve with the warm apricot sauce.

Poached Salmon with Hollandaise Sauce

Serves 8

ingredients

- melted butter, for greasing
- 1.8 kg/4 lb whole fresh salmon, gutted
- 1 lemon, sliced
- sprigs of fresh parsley
- 125 ml/4 fl oz white wine or water
- salt and pepper
- lemon wedges, to serve
- sprigs of fresh parsley, to garnish

hollandaise sauce

- 2 tbsp white wine vinegar
- 2 tbsp water
- 6 black peppercorns
- 3 egg yolks
- 250 g/9 oz unsalted butter
- 2 tsp lemon juice
- salt and pepper

1 Preheat the oven to 150ºC/300ºF/ Gas Mark 2. Line a large roasting tin with a double layer of foil and brush with butter.

2 Trim off the fins then season the salmon with salt and pepper, inside and out. Lay on the foil and place the lemon slices and parsley in the body cavity. Pour over the wine and gather up the foil to make a fairly loose parcel.

3 Place the tin in the preheated oven and bake for 50–60 minutes. Test the salmon with the point of a knife: the flesh should flake when the fish is cooked. Remove from the oven and leave to stand for 15 minutes before removing from the foil to serve hot. To serve cold, leave for 1–2 hours until lukewarm, then carefully remove from the foil and peel away the skin from the top side, leaving the head and tail intact.

4 Meanwhile, to make the hollandaise sauce, put the vinegar and water into a small saucepan with the peppercorns, bring to the boil, then reduce the heat and simmer until it is reduced to 1 tablespoon (take care: this happens very quickly), then strain.

5 Mix the egg yolks in a blender or food processor and add the strained vinegar while the machine is running.

6 Melt the butter in a small saucepan and heat until it almost turns brown. Again, while the blender is running, add three quarters of the butter, the lemon juice and the remaining butter and season well with salt and pepper.

7 Turn the sauce into a serving bowl or keep warm for up to 1 hour in a bowl over a saucepan of warm water. To serve cold, leave to cool and store in the refrigerator for up to 2 days.

8 Serve the salmon garnished with parsley, and with lemon wedges and Hollandaise sauce on the side.

Griddled Scallops with Crispy Leeks

Serves 6

ingredients
- 6 chunky leeks
- 50 g/1¾ oz butter
- 1 scant tsp set honey
- sunflower oil, for deep-frying
- 1 tsp sea salt flakes
- 18 plump raw scallops, shelled and cleaned
- 1–2 tbsp olive oil
- freshly squeezed lemon juice, to taste
- salt and pepper

1 Trim the leeks and roughly chop five of them. Halve the remaining leek, cut into very fine julienne strips and reserve. Heat the butter in a frying pan over a medium heat, add the chopped leeks and cook, stirring frequently, for 5 minutes, or until soft but not coloured. Add the honey, season to taste with salt and pepper and keep warm.

2 Meanwhile, heat the oil for deep-frying in a deep-fat fryer or wok to 180–190°C/350–375°F, or until a cube of bread browns in 30 seconds. Add the leek julienne to the hot oil and cook until crisp and golden. Remove with a slotted spoon and drain on kitchen paper. Lightly scatter with the sea salt flakes.

3 Heat a ridged griddle pan over a high heat. Brush the scallops with the olive oil, add to the pan and cook for a little over 1 minute on each side. Remove from the heat and season with lemon juice to taste and a light sprinkling of salt.

4 Place a dollop of buttered leeks onto each of six warmed serving plates, top each with 3 scallops, add a tangle of crispy leeks and serve immediately.

Garlic & Herb
Dublin Bay Prawns

Serves 2

ingredients

- 12 raw Dublin Bay prawns in their shells
- juice of ½ lemon
- 2 garlic cloves, crushed
- 3 tbsp chopped fresh parsley, plus extra to garnish
- 1 tbsp chopped fresh dill
- 3 tbsp softened butter
- salt and pepper
- lemon wedges and crusty bread, to serve

1 Rinse and peel the prawns. Devein, using a sharp knife to slice along the back from the head end to the tail, and remove the thin black intestine.

2 Mix the lemon juice with the garlic, herbs and butter to form a paste. Season well with salt and pepper. Spread the paste over the prawns and leave to marinate for 30 minutes.

3 Meanwhile, preheat the grill to medium. Cook the prawns under the preheated grill for 5–6 minutes. Alternatively, heat a frying pan, add the prawns and fry until cooked. Turn out onto hot plates and pour over the pan juices. Scatter over some chopped parsley and serve at once with lemon wedges and some crusty bread.

Mixed Nut Roast with Cranberry & Red Wine Sauce

Serves 4

ingredients

- 2 tbsp butter, plus extra for greasing
- 2 garlic cloves, chopped
- 1 large onion, chopped
- 50 g/1¾ oz pine kernels, toasted
- 75 g/2¾ oz hazelnuts, toasted
- 50 g/1¾ oz walnuts, ground
- 50 g/1¾ oz cashew nuts, ground
- 100 g/3½ oz wholemeal breadcrumbs
- 1 egg, lightly beaten
- 2 tbsp chopped fresh thyme
- 250 ml/9 fl oz vegetable stock
- salt and pepper
- sprigs of fresh thyme, to garnish

cranberry & red wine sauce

- 175 g/6 oz fresh cranberries
- 100 g/3½ oz caster sugar
- 300 ml/10 fl oz red wine
- 1 cinnamon stick

1 Preheat the oven to 180°C/350°F/ Gas Mark 4. Grease a loaf tin and line with greaseproof paper. Melt the butter in a saucepan over a medium heat. Add the garlic and onion and cook, stirring, for about 3 minutes.

2 Remove the pan from the heat. Grind the pine kernels, hazelnuts, walnuts and cashews and stir into the pan. Add the breadcrumbs, egg, thyme, stock and seasoning.

3 Spoon the mixture into the loaf tin and level the surface. Cook in the centre of the preheated oven for 30 minutes or until cooked through and golden. The loaf is cooked when a skewer inserted into the centre comes out clean.

4 Halfway through the cooking time, make the sauce. Put all the ingredients in a saucepan and bring to the boil. Reduce the heat and simmer, stirring occasionally, for 15 minutes.

5 Remove the nut roast from the oven and turn out. Garnish with sprigs of thyme and serve with the sauce.

Chapter 5
Weekend Wonders

Roast Beef

Serves 8

ingredients

- 1 prime rib of beef joint, weighing 2.7 kg/6 lb
- 2 tsp English mustard powder
- 3 tbsp plain flour
- 300 ml/10 fl oz red wine
- 300 ml/10 fl oz beef stock
- 2 tsp Worcestershire sauce (optional)
- salt and pepper
- Yorkshire Puddings (see page 74) and a selection of vegetables, to serve

1 Preheat the oven to 230°C/450°F/ Gas Mark 8. Season the meat to taste with salt and pepper. Rub in the mustard and 1 tablespoon of the flour.

2 Place the meat in a roasting tin large enough to hold it comfortably and roast in the preheated oven for 15 minutes. Reduce the temperature to 190°C/375°F/ Gas Mark 5 and cook for 15 minutes per 450 g/1 lb, plus 15 minutes (1¾ hours for this joint) for rare, or 20 minutes per 450 g/ 1 lb, plus 20 minutes (2 hours 20 minutes for this joint) for medium. Baste the meat from time to time to keep it moist, and if the tin becomes too dry, add a little stock or wine.

3 Remove the meat from the oven and place on a warmed serving plate, cover with foil and leave in a warm place for 10–15 minutes.

4 To make the gravy, pour off most of the fat from the tin (reserve it for cooking the Yorkshire Pudding), leaving behind the meat juices and the sediment. Place the tin on the hob over a medium heat and scrape all the sediment from the base of the tin. Sprinkle in the remaining flour and quickly mix it into the juices with a small whisk. When you have a smooth paste, gradually add the wine and most of the stock, whisking constantly. Bring to the boil, then reduce the heat to a gentle simmer and cook for 2–3 minutes. Season to taste with salt and pepper and add the remaining stock, if needed, and a little Worcestershire sauce, if using.

5 When ready to serve, carve the meat into slices and serve on warmed plates. Pour the gravy into a warmed jug and place on the table. Serve the beef with Yorkshire Puddings and a selection of vegetables.

Roast Leg of Lamb

Serves 6

ingredients
- 1.5 kg/3 lb 5 oz leg of lamb
- 6 garlic cloves, thinly sliced lengthways
- 8 fresh rosemary sprigs
- 4 tbsp olive oil
- salt and pepper

glaze
- 4 tbsp redcurrant jelly
- 300 ml/10 fl oz rosé wine

1 Preheat the oven to 200°C/400°F/ Gas Mark 6. Using a small knife, cut slits all over the leg of lamb. Insert 1–2 garlic slices and 4–5 rosemary needles in each slit. Place any remaining rosemary in the base of a roasting tin. Season the lamb to taste with salt and pepper and place in the roasting tin. Pour over the oil. Cover with foil and roast in the preheated oven for 1 hour 20 minutes.

2 Mix the redcurrant jelly and wine together in a small saucepan. Heat gently, stirring constantly, until combined. Bring to the boil, then reduce the heat and simmer until reduced.

3 Remove the lamb from the oven and pour over the glaze. Return to the oven and cook, uncovered, for about 10 minutes, depending on how well done you like it.

4 Remove the lamb from the roasting tin, cover with foil and leave to rest for 15 minutes before carving and serving.

Shepherd's Pie

Serves 6

ingredients

- 1 tbsp olive oil
- 2 onions, finely chopped
- 2 garlic cloves, finely chopped
- 675 g/1 lb 8 oz good-quality minced lamb
- 2 carrots, finely chopped
- 1 tbsp plain flour
- 225 ml/8 fl oz beef stock or chicken stock
- 125 ml/4 fl oz red wine
- Worcestershire sauce (optional)
- salt and pepper

mashed potato topping

- 675 g/1 lb 8 oz floury potatoes, such as King Edward, Maris Piper or Desirée, peeled and cut into chunks
- 55 g/2 oz butter
- 2 tbsp cream or milk
- salt and pepper

1 Preheat the oven to 180°C/350°F/ Gas Mark 4.

2 Heat the oil in a large flameproof casserole dish, add the onions and fry until soft, then add the garlic and stir well.

3 Increase the heat and add the meat. Cook quickly to brown the meat all over, stirring constantly. Add the carrots and season well with salt and pepper.

4 Stir in the flour and add the stock and wine. Stir well and heat until simmering and thickened.

5 Cover the casserole dish and cook in the oven for about 1 hour. Check the consistency from time to time and add a little more stock or wine if required. The meat mixture should be quite thick but not dry. Season to taste with salt and pepper and add a little Worcestershire sauce, if using.

6 While the meat is cooking, make the mashed potato topping. Bring a large saucepan of lightly salted water to the boil, add the potatoes and cook for 15–20 minutes. Drain well and mash with a potato masher until smooth. Add the butter and cream and season well with salt and pepper.

7 Spoon the lamb mixture into an ovenproof serving dish and spread or pipe the potato on top.

8 Increase the oven temperature to 200°C/400°F/Gas Mark 6 and cook the pie for 15–20 minutes at the top of the oven until golden brown. You might like to finish it off under a medium grill for a really crisp brown topping to the potato. Serve on warmed plates.

Toad-In-The-Hole

Serves 4

ingredients
- oil, for greasing
- 115 g/4 oz plain flour
- pinch of salt
- 1 egg, beaten
- 300 ml/10 fl oz milk
- 450 g/1 lb good-quality pork sausages
- 1 tbsp vegetable oil

1 Grease a 20 x 25-cm/8 x 10-inch ovenproof dish or roasting tin.

2 Make the batter by sifting the flour and salt into a mixing bowl. Make a well in the centre and add the beaten egg and half the milk. Carefully stir the liquid into the flour until the mixture is smooth. Gradually beat in the remaining milk. Leave to stand for 30 minutes.

3 Preheat the oven to 220°C/425°F/Gas Mark 7. Prick the sausages and place them in the prepared dish. Sprinkle over the oil and cook in the preheated oven for 10 minutes until the sausages are beginning to colour and the fat has started to run and is sizzling.

4 Remove from the oven and quickly pour the batter over the sausages. Return to the oven and cook for 35–45 minutes until the batter is well risen and golden brown. Serve immediately.

Roast Pork with Crackling

Serves 4

ingredients
- 1 kg/2 lb 4 oz piece of pork loin, boned and the skin removed and reserved
- 2 tbsp mustard
- salt and pepper

gravy
- 1 tbsp flour
- 300 ml/10 fl oz cider, apple juice or stock

apple sauce
- 450 g/1 lb Bramley apples, peeled, cored and sliced
- 3 tablespoons water
- 15 g/½ oz caster sugar
- pinch of ground cinnamon (optional)
- 15 g/½ oz butter (optional)

1 To make the apple sauce, put the apples into a medium-sized saucepan. Add the water and sugar and cook over a gentle heat for 10 minutes, stirring from time to time. Add the cinnamon and butter, if using. Beat well until the sauce is thick and smooth.

2 Preheat the oven to 200°C/400°F/ Gas Mark 6. Make sure the skin of the pork is well scored and sprinkle it with the salt. Place on a wire rack on a baking tray and roast for 30–40 minutes until the crackling is golden brown and crispy. This can be cooked in advance, leaving room in the oven for roast potatoes.

3 Season the loin of pork with salt and pepper and spread the fat with the mustard. Place in a roasting tin and roast in the centre of the oven for about 20 minutes. Reduce the oven temperature to 190°C/375°F/Gas Mark 5 and cook for 50–60 minutes until the meat is a good colour and the juices run clear when pierced with a skewer.

4 Remove the meat from the oven and place on a warmed serving plate, cover with foil and leave to rest in a warm place.

5 To make the gravy, pour off most of the fat from the roasting tin, leaving the meat juices and the sediment. Sprinkle in the flour, whisking well. Cook the paste for a couple of minutes, then add the cider a little at a time until you have a smooth gravy. Boil for 2–3 minutes until it is the required consistency. Season well with salt and pepper and pour into a warmed serving jug.

6 Carve the pork into slices and serve on warmed plates with pieces of the crackling and the gravy. Serve the sauce on the side.

Chicken, Mushroom
& Tarragon Pie

Serves 4–6

ingredients

- 1 chicken, about 1.5 kg/3 lb 5 oz
- 2 fresh tarragon sprigs
- 1 Spanish onion, cut into wedges
- 25 g/1 oz butter
- 175 g/6 oz chestnut mushrooms, sliced
- 2 tbsp plain flour
- 55 g/2 oz frozen peas or shelled fresh peas
- 1 tbsp chopped fresh tarragon
- salt and pepper

pastry

- 225 g/8 oz plain flour, plus extra for dusting
- 175 g/6 oz butter
- 4 tbsp iced water
- 1 egg, lightly beaten
- salt

1 Preheat the oven to 200°C/400°F/ Gas Mark 6. Put the chicken, tarragon sprigs and onion into a casserole, add 300 ml/10 fl oz water and season with salt and pepper. Cover and bake in the preheated oven for 1½ hours. Remove from the oven and lift out the chicken from the casserole. Strain the cooking juices into a measuring jug and chill.

2 Meanwhile, make the pastry. Sift the flour with a pinch of salt into a bowl and add the butter and water. Mix to a firm but slightly lumpy dough, adding more iced water if necessary. Roll out into a rectangle on a floured surface, then fold the top third down and the bottom third up. Give the dough a quarter turn, roll out and fold again. Repeat once more, then wrap and chill.

3 Discard the chicken skin, cut off the meat and dice. Skim off the fat from the cooking juices and make up to 300 ml/ 10 fl oz with water.

4 Melt the butter in a large saucepan. Cook the mushrooms over a medium heat for 3 minutes. Stir in the flour for 1 minute, then gradually stir in the cooking juices. Bring to the boil, add the chicken, peas and tarragon and season. Transfer to a pie dish and leave to cool.

5 Preheat the oven to 200°C/400°F/ Gas Mark 6. Roll out the pastry to 2.5 cm/1 inch larger than the top of the dish. Cut out a 15-mm/⅝-inch strip all the way around. Brush the rim of the dish with water and press the strip onto it. Brush with water and lift the remaining dough on top. Trim off the excess and crimp the edges to seal. Make a slit in the centre and brush with beaten egg. Roll out the trimmings and use to decorate the pie, then brush with beaten egg. Bake for 40 minutes until golden. Serve immediately.

Roast Chicken

Serves 6

ingredients
- 2.25 kg/5 lb free-range chicken
- 55 g/2 oz butter
- 2 tbsp chopped fresh lemon thyme
- 1 lemon, quartered
- 125 ml/4 fl oz white wine
- salt and pepper
- 6 sprigs of fresh thyme, to garnish

1 Preheat the oven to 220°C/425°F/ Gas Mark 7.

2 Wipe the chicken well with kitchen paper, inside and out, and place in a roasting tin.

3 Place the butter in a bowl and soften with a fork, then mix in the herbs and season well with salt and pepper.

4 Butter the chicken all over with the herb butter, inside and out, and place the lemon pieces inside the body cavity. Pour the wine over the chicken.

5 Roast in the centre of the preheated oven for 20 minutes. Reduce the temperature to 190°C/375°F/ Gas Mark 5 and continue to roast for a further 1¼ hours, basting frequently. Cover with foil if the skin begins to brown too much. If the tin dries out, add a little more wine or water.

6 Test that the chicken is cooked by piercing the thickest part of the leg with a sharp knife or skewer and making sure the juices run clear. Remove from the oven.

7 Remove the chicken from the roasting tin and place on a warmed serving plate, cover with foil and leave to rest for 10 minutes before carving.

8 Place the roasting tin on the hob over a low heat and bubble the pan juices gently until they have reduced and are thick and glossy. Season with salt and pepper.

9 Serve the chicken with the pan juices and scatter with the thyme sprigs.

Fish & Chips

Serves 2

ingredients

- vegetable oil, for deep-frying
- 3 large potatoes, such as Cara or Desirée
- 2 thick cod or haddock fillets, 175 g/6 oz each
- 175 g/6 oz self-raising flour, plus extra for dusting
- 200 ml/7 fl oz cold lager
- salt and pepper
- tartare sauce, to serve

1 Heat the oil in a temperature-controlled deep-fat fryer to 120ºC/250ºF, or in a heavy-based saucepan, checking the temperature with a thermometer, to blanch the chips. Preheat the oven to 150°C/300°F/Gas Mark 2.

2 Peel the potatoes and cut into even-sized chips. Fry for about 8–10 minutes, depending on size, until soft but not coloured. Remove from the oil, drain on kitchen paper and place in a warmed dish in the preheated oven. Increase the temperature of the oil to 180–190ºC/350–375ºF, or until a cube of bread browns in 30 seconds.

3 Meanwhile, season the fish with salt and pepper and dust lightly with flour.

4 Make a thick batter by sifting the flour into a bowl with a little salt and whisking in most of the lager. Check the consistency of the batter before adding the remaining lager: it should be very thick like double cream.

5 Dip one fillet into the batter and allow the batter to coat it thickly. Carefully place the fish in the hot oil, then repeat with the other fillet.

6 Cook for 8–10 minutes, depending on the thickness of the fish. Turn over the fillets halfway through the cooking time. Remove the fish from the fryer, drain and keep warm.

7 Make sure the oil temperature is still at 180ºC/350ºF and return the chips to the fryer. Cook for a further 2–3 minutes until golden brown and crispy. Drain and season with salt and pepper before serving with the battered fish and tartare sauce.

Fish Cakes

Serves 4

ingredients

- 450 g/1 lb floury potatoes, such as King Edward, Maris Piper or Desirée, peeled and cut into chunks
- 450 g/1lb mixed fish fillets, such as cod and salmon, skinned
- 2 tbsp chopped fresh tarragon
- grated rind of 1 lemon
- 2 tbsp double cream
- 1 tbsp plain flour
- 1 egg, beaten
- 115 g/4 oz breadcrumbs, made from day-old white bread or wholemeal bread
- salt and pepper
- 4 tbsp vegetable oil, for frying
- watercress salad and lemon wedges, to serve

1 Bring a large saucepan of lightly salted water to the boil, add the potatoes and cook for 15–20 minutes. Drain well and mash with a potato masher until smooth.

2 Place the fish in a frying pan and just cover with water. Bring to the boil over a medium heat, then reduce the heat, cover the pan and simmer gently for 5 minutes until cooked.

3 Remove the pan from the heat and drain the fish onto a plate. When cool enough to handle, flake the fish roughly into good-sized pieces, ensuring that there are no bones.

4 Mix the potato with the fish, tarragon, lemon rind and cream. Season well with salt and pepper and shape into four round cakes or eight smaller ones.

5 Dust the cakes with flour and dip them into the beaten egg, then coat thoroughly with the breadcrumbs. Place on a baking tray and leave to chill for at least 30 minutes.

6 Heat the oil in the pan, add the cakes and fry over a medium heat for 5 minutes on each side, turning them carefully with a palette knife or a fish slice.

7 Serve immediately with a watercress salad and lemon wedges.

Star-gazy Pie

Serves 4–6

ingredients

- 85 g/3 oz fresh breadcrumbs
- 4 tbsp milk
- 2 tbsp freshly chopped parsley and thyme
- juice and grated rind of 1 lemon
- 1 onion, chopped
- 115 g/4 oz lardons or streaky bacon, cut into strips
- 6 pilchards or large sardines, gutted and deboned, with the heads left on
- 2 hard-boiled eggs, chopped
- 150 ml/5 fl oz cider or apple juice
- 225 g/8 oz shortcrust pastry
- 1 egg, beaten to glaze
- salt and pepper
- seasonal green vegetables, to serve

1 Preheat the oven to 200°C/400°F/ Gas Mark 6.

2 Soak the breadcrumbs in the milk. Add the herbs, lemon juice and rind.

3 Fry the onion and bacon in a non-stick frying pan for 4–5 minutes, until the onions are soft and the bacon is cooked. Add half the mixture to the breadcrumbs and season well. Use to stuff the fish.

4 Arrange the fish in a 23-cm/9-inch pie dish with the tails down and the heads pointing over the edges of the dish. Scatter the remaining onion mixture and the chopped eggs in between the fish. Season and pour in the cider.

5 Roll out the pastry just larger than the dish and place a strip around the rim of the pie dish. Brush the pastry with water and cover the whole dish, allowing the fish heads to poke through on the rim. Glaze the pastry with the beaten egg and bake the pie for 40–45 minutes until the pastry is golden brown. Reduce the temperature if the pastry gets too brown or cover the pie with foil. Serve hot with vegetables.

Perfect Macaroni Cheese

Serves 4

ingredients

- 250 g/9 oz dried macaroni pasta
- 55 g/2 oz butter, plus extra for cooking the pasta
- 600 ml/1 pint milk
- ½ tsp grated nutmeg
- 55 g/2 oz plain flour
- 200 g/7 oz mature Cheddar cheese, grated
- 55 g/2 oz Parmesan cheese, grated
- 200 g/7 oz baby spinach
- salt and pepper

1 Cook the macaroni according to the instructions on the packet. Remove from the heat, drain, add a small knob of butter to keep it soft, return to the saucepan and cover to keep warm.

2 Put the milk and nutmeg into a saucepan over a low heat and heat until warm, but don't boil. Put the butter into a heavy-based saucepan over a low heat, melt the butter, add the flour and stir to make a roux. Cook gently for 2 minutes. Add the milk a little at a time, whisking it into the roux, then cook for about 10–15 minutes to make a loose, custard-style sauce.

3 Add three quarters of the Cheddar cheese and Parmesan cheese and stir through until they have melted in, then add the spinach, season to taste with salt and pepper and remove from the heat.

4 Preheat the grill to high. Put the macaroni into a shallow heatproof dish, then pour the sauce over. Scatter the remaining cheese over the top and place the dish under the preheated grill. Grill until the cheese begins to brown, then serve.

Chapter 6
Vegetables & Sides

Perfect Roast Potatoes

Serves 6

ingredients
- 1.3 kg/3 lb large floury potatoes, such as King Edward, Maris Piper or Desirée, peeled and cut into even-sized chunks
- 3 tbsp dripping, goose fat, duck fat or olive oil
- salt

1 Preheat the oven to 220ºC/425ºF/ Gas Mark 7.

2 Bring a large saucepan of lightly salted water to the boil, add the potatoes and cook over a medium heat, covered, for 5–7 minutes. They will still be firm. Remove from the heat.

3 Meanwhile, add the fat to a roasting tin and place in the preheated oven.

4 Drain the potatoes well and return them to the pan. Cover with the lid and firmly shake the pan so that the surface of the potatoes is roughened. This will help give a much crisper texture.

5 Remove the tin from the oven and carefully tip the potatoes into the hot oil. Baste them to ensure they are all coated with the oil.

6 Roast at the top of the oven for 45–50 minutes until they are browned all over and thoroughly crisp. Turn the potatoes and baste again only once during the process or the crunchy edges will be destroyed.

7 Carefully transfer the potatoes from the tin into a warmed serving dish. Sprinkle with a little salt and serve at once.

Champ

Serves 4

ingredients

- 900 g/2 lb potatoes
- 2 bunches of spring onions
- 200 ml/7 fl oz milk or single cream
- 55 g/2 oz butter, plus extra for serving
- salt and pepper
- 2 tbsp chopped chives and 2 tbsp chopped parsley, to garnish

1 Peel the potatoes and cut into large chunks. Bring a large saucepan of water to the boil, add the potatoes and cook for 15–20 minutes until tender.

2 Cut the spring onions into 1-cm/½-inch slices.

3 Drain the potatoes well and mash with a potato masher. If you want very smooth champ you could press them through a sieve. Keep warm.

4 Melt the butter in a medium-sized saucepan and add the spring onions. Sweat for 3–4 minutes until soft. Add the milk or cream and bring to a simmer, season well and allow to thicken slightly.

5 Stir the onion mixture into the warm potatoes and adjust the seasoning, if necessary. Scatter over the chopped herbs and serve immediately, with extra butter on the side. Delicious as an accompaniment to beef, lamb and venison.

Honeyed Parsnips

Serves 4

ingredients
- 8 parsnips, peeled and quartered
- 4 tbsp vegetable oil
- 1 tbsp honey

1 Preheat the oven to 180°C/350°F/ Gas Mark 4.

2 Bring a large saucepan of water to the boil. Reduce the heat, add the parsnips and cook for 5 minutes. Drain thoroughly.

3 Pour 2 tablespoons of the oil into a shallow, ovenproof dish and add the parsnips. Mix the remaining oil with the honey and drizzle over the parsnips. Roast in the preheated oven for 45 minutes until golden brown and tender. Remove from the oven and serve.

Cauliflower Cheese

Serves 4

ingredients
- 675 g/1 lb 8 oz cauliflower florets
- 40 g/1½ oz butter
- 40 g/1½ oz plain flour
- 450 ml/16 fl oz milk
- 115 g/4 oz Cheddar cheese, finely grated
- whole nutmeg, for grating
- 1 tbsp grated Parmesan cheese
- salt and pepper

1 Bring a saucepan of lightly salted water to the boil, add the cauliflower and cook for 4–5 minutes. It should still be firm. Drain, place in a warmed 4-litre/2½-pint gratin dish and keep warm.

2 Melt the butter in the rinsed-out saucepan over a medium heat, stir in the flour and cook for 1 minute, stirring the mixture constantly.

3 Remove from the heat and stir in the milk very gradually until the consistency is smooth.

4 Return to a medium heat and continue to stir while the sauce comes to the boil and thickens. Reduce the heat and simmer gently, stirring constantly, for about 3 minutes, until the sauce is creamy and smooth.

5 Remove from the heat and stir in the Cheddar cheese and a good grating of nutmeg. Taste and season well with salt and pepper.

6 Pour the hot cheese sauce over the cauliflower, top with the Parmesan cheese and place under a hot grill to brown. Serve immediately.

Brussels Sprouts with Buttered Chestnuts

Serves 4

ingredients

- 350 g/12 oz Brussels sprouts, trimmed
- 3 tbsp butter
- 100 g/3½ oz canned whole chestnuts
- pinch of nutmeg
- salt and pepper
- 50 g/1¾ oz flaked almonds, to garnish

1 Bring a large saucepan of water to the boil. Add the Brussels sprouts and cook for 5 minutes. Drain thoroughly.

2 Melt the butter in a large saucepan over a medium heat. Add the Brussels sprouts and cook, stirring, for 3 minutes.

3 Add the chestnuts and nutmeg to the pan. Season with salt and pepper and stir well. Cook for a further 2 minutes, stirring, then remove from the heat.

4 Transfer to a serving dish, scatter over the almonds and serve.

Ways with Mushrooms

Finding mushrooms growing wild is a real joy. If you've got a good eye and you know which varieties are edible, you can go out for a walk in the morning and come home with your breakfast, lunch or dinner. Sadly, these days it is not often you come across enough mushrooms to take home to cook. Luckily we can now find many varieties of mushrooms in the supermarkets that are cultivated, available throughout the year and can be used in a variety of dishes.

Mushrooms in Red Wine

Heat 25 g/1 oz butter in a frying pan, add 4 finely chopped shallots and 2 finely chopped garlic cloves. Cook for 1–2 minutes until the shallots are soft. Add 100 g/ 3½ oz whole shiitake mushrooms and the same weight of whole small chestnut mushrooms to the pan and stir well. Add 175 ml/6 fl oz beef stock or vegetable stock and 175 ml/6 fl oz red wine with 1 tablespoon chopped fresh thyme and leave to simmer until the sauce has reduced by half and the mushrooms are soft. Serve immediately. This can be served as a starter or as an accompaniment to steak. Serves 3–4.

Baked Mushrooms

Preheat the oven to 200°C/400°F/ Gas Mark 6. Wipe 4 large flat mushrooms and cut out their stalks. Place the mushrooms in a baking dish and sprinkle over 2 finely chopped garlic cloves and 1 tablespoon finely chopped fresh thyme. Spoon in 4 tablespoons melted butter and squeeze in the juice of 1 lemon. Drizzle over 2 tablespoons olive oil and bake in the oven for 20–25 minutes, basting from time to time. These can be served with couscous or rice to make a good vegetarian supper dish, or with grilled meats or simply on toast. Serves 2.

Mushroom Risotto

Fry 55 g/2 oz chopped streaky bacon in a large frying pan with 1 finely chopped onion, 25 g/1 oz butter and 1 tablespoon olive oil until the onion is a pale golden colour and the bacon has started to brown. Add 350 g/12 oz risotto rice and stir well. Have ready 1 litre/ 1¾ pints hot vegetable stock and slowly add a ladleful to the rice. Allow the rice to absorb the stock before adding the next ladleful, stirring constantly. Continue slowly adding stock until it is all used up: this will take 15–20 minutes. Stir in 175 g/6 oz sliced mushrooms. (It is nice to use more exotic ones, such as ceps, morels or shiitake, if you can find them. Otherwise use chestnut or field mushrooms.) Allow to cook until the mushrooms have reduced and softened and the rice is just soft. Add a further 25 g/1 oz butter to the pan and season to taste with salt and pepper. Serve in warmed bowls garnished with freshly chopped parsley. Serves 3–4.

Bubble & Squeak

Serves 2–3

ingredients

- 450 g/1 lb floury potatoes, such as King Edward, Maris Piper or Desirée, peeled and cut into chunks
- 55 g/2 oz butter
- 3 tbsp hot milk
- 450 g/1 lb green cabbage
- 4 tbsp olive oil
- 1 onion, thinly sliced
- salt and pepper

1 Bring a large saucepan of lightly salted water to the boil, add the potatoes and cook for 15–20 minutes. Drain well and mash with a potato masher until smooth. Season with salt and pepper, add the butter and milk and stir well.

2 Cut the cabbage into quarters, remove the stalk and finely shred the leaves.

3 Put half the oil into a large frying pan, add the onion and fry until soft. Add the cabbage to the pan and stir-fry for 2–3 minutes until soft. Season with salt and pepper, add the potato and mix together well.

4 Press the mixture firmly into the frying pan and leave to cook over a high heat for 4–5 minutes until the base is crispy. Place a plate over the pan and invert the pan so that the potato cake falls onto the plate. Add the remaining oil to the pan, reheat and slip the cake back into the pan with the uncooked side down.

5 Continue to cook for a further 5 minutes until the base is crispy. Turn out onto a warmed plate and cut into wedges for serving. Serve immediately.

Neeps & Tatties

Serves 4–5

ingredients
- 450 g/1 lb swedes, peeled and diced
- 250 g/9 oz floury potatoes, such as King Edward, Maris Piper or Desirée, peeled and diced
- 55 g/2 oz butter
- whole nutmeg, for grating
- salt and pepper
- fresh parsley sprigs, to garnish

1 Bring a large saucepan of lightly salted water to the boil, add the swedes and potatoes and cook for 20 minutes until soft. Test with the point of a knife – if not cooked return to the heat for a further 5 minutes.

2 Drain well, return to the rinsed-out pan and heat for a few moments to ensure they are dry. Mash with a potato masher until smooth. Season well with salt and pepper and add the butter. Grate nutmeg into the mash to taste and serve piping hot, garnished with the parsley.

Braised Red Cabbage

Serves 6

ingredients
- 2 tbsp sunflower oil
- 2 onions, thinly sliced
- 2 eating apples, peeled, cored and thinly sliced
- 900 g/2 lb red cabbage, cored and shredded
- 4 tbsp red wine vinegar
- 2 tbsp sugar
- ¼ tsp ground cloves
- 55 g/2 oz raisins
- 125 ml/4 fl oz red wine
- 2 tbsp redcurrant jelly
- salt and pepper

1 Heat the oil in a large saucepan. Add the onions and cook, stirring occasionally, for 10 minutes, or until soft and golden. Stir in the apple slices and cook for 3 minutes.

2 Add the cabbage, vinegar, sugar, cloves, raisins and red wine and season to taste with salt and pepper. Bring to the boil, stirring occasionally.

3 Reduce the heat, cover and cook, stirring occasionally, for 40 minutes, or until the cabbage is tender and most of the liquid has been absorbed.

4 Stir in the redcurrant jelly, transfer to a warmed dish and serve.

Roasted Onions

Serves 4

ingredients
- 8 large onions, peeled
- 3 tbsp olive oil
- 55 g/2 oz butter
- 2 tsp chopped fresh thyme
- 200 g/7 oz Cheddar cheese or Lancashire cheese, grated
- salt and pepper
- salad and crusty bread, to serve

1 Preheat the oven to 180°C/350°F/Gas Mark 4.

2 Cut a cross down through the top of the onions towards the root, without cutting all the way through.

3 Place the onions in a roasting tin and drizzle over the olive oil.

4 Press a little of the butter into the open crosses, sprinkle with the thyme and season with salt and pepper. Cover with foil and roast in the preheated oven for 40–45 minutes.

5 Remove from the oven, take off the foil and baste the onions with the pan juices. Return to the oven and cook for a further 15 minutes, uncovered, to allow the onions to brown.

6 Take the onions out of the oven and scatter the grated cheese over them. Return them to the oven for a few minutes so that the cheese starts to melt.

7 Serve at once with some salad and lots of warm crusty bread.

Roasted Root Vegetables

Serves 4–6

ingredients

- 3 parsnips, peeled and cut into 5-cm/2-inch pieces
- 4 baby turnips, quartered
- 3 carrots, peeled and cut into 5-cm/2-inch pieces
- 450 g/1 lb butternut squash, peeled and cut into 5-cm/2-inch chunks
- 450 g/1 lb sweet potato, peeled and cut into 5-cm/2-inch chunks
- 2 garlic cloves, finely chopped
- 2 tbsp chopped fresh rosemary
- 2 tbsp chopped fresh thyme
- 2 tsp chopped fresh sage
- 3 tbsp olive oil
- salt and pepper
- 2 tbsp chopped fresh mixed herbs, such as parsley, thyme and mint, to garnish

1 Preheat the oven to 220°C/425°F/ Gas Mark 7.

2 Arrange all the vegetables in a single layer in a large roasting tin. Scatter over the garlic and the herbs.

3 Pour over the oil and season well with salt and pepper.

4 Toss all the ingredients together until they are well mixed and coated with the oil (you can leave them to marinate at this stage to allow the flavours to be absorbed).

5 Roast at the top of the preheated oven for 50–60 minutes until the vegetables are cooked and nicely browned. Turn the vegetables over halfway through the cooking time.

6 Serve with a good handful of fresh herbs scattered on top and a final sprinkling of salt and pepper.

Asparagus with Melted Butter

Serves 2

ingredients
- 16–20 asparagus stalks, trimmed to about 20 cm/8 inches
- 85 g/3 oz unsalted butter, melted
- salt and pepper, to serve

1 Remove some of the base of the asparagus stalks with a potato peeler if they are rather thick.

2 Tie the stalks together with string or put them into a wire basket so that they can easily be removed from the cooking water without being damaged.

3 Bring a large saucepan of lightly salted water to the boil and plunge in the stalks. Cover with a lid and cook for 4–5 minutes.

4 Pierce one stalk near the base with a sharp knife to test. If it is fairly soft remove from the heat at once. Do not overcook asparagus or the tender tips will fall off.

5 Drain the asparagus thoroughly and serve on large warmed plates with the butter poured over or in a separate bowl for dipping. Both the butter and the asparagus should be warm rather than hot. Serve with salt and pepper and hand out large napkins!

Garden Salads & Herbs

Today new varieties of 'designer' salad leaves can be found everywhere and we no longer have to have a plain salad of lettuce, tomato and cucumber on our plates. Herbs have always been grown in Britain, but now there is a renewed interest in using them and we are able to buy many more varieties than before, which means we can add interesting twists and flavours to our salads and other dishes. Particularly useful are the herbs sold in pots, which give us a fresh supply for days at a time.

Simple Garden Salad

Take a handful of rocket and trim away any particularly long stems. Pick over a handful of lamb's lettuce and mizuna and tear some leaves of frisée into small pieces. Wash if necessary and dry thoroughly. Place the salad leaves in a bowl and add a mixture of herbs, such as parsley, chervil and a few leaves of lemon thyme. Sprinkle over 2–3 tablespoons olive oil and 1 teaspoon freshly squeezed lemon juice and toss to coat the leaves. Season with salt and pepper, toss again and serve. Serves 4.

Tomato Salad

A mixture of tomato varieties in a salad is good as it looks colourful and adds different flavours. Slice 2 beefsteak tomatoes horizontally and cut 4 plum tomatoes into quarters. Cut 12 red cherry tomatoes in half and the same number of gold cherry tomatoes (about 600 g/1 lb 5 oz tomatoes in total). Arrange the tomatoes in a shallow dish, sprinkle with ½ teaspoon salt and ½ teaspoon of sugar and pour over 5 tablespoons olive oil. Scatter with a good handful of shredded basil and leave to stand for 30 minutes before serving to allow the flavours to mingle. Serves 4.

Special Potato Salad

The first waxy salad potatoes of the season are ideal for making a potato salad. Scrub 800 g/1 lb 12 oz small potatoes. Bring a large saucepan of lightly salted water to the boil, add the potatoes and cook for 15–20 minutes until tender. Drain and halve the potatoes while still warm. Place in a serving dish and add 3 tablespoons chopped fresh mixed herbs (parsley, chives, basil and chervil). Pour over 6 tablespoons olive oil and 2 tablespoons white wine, season well with salt and pepper and toss the contents of the dish together. Serve while still warm. If you prefer, you could use a dressing of sour cream or crème fraîche. Serves 4.

Good Coleslaw

Shred half a hard white cabbage finely. Grate 2 carrots and core and slice 2 green apples. Chop 2 celery sticks and 3 spring onions finely. Place all the ingredients in a large bowl. In a small bowl, mix together 150 ml/5 fl oz mayonnaise and the same quantity of natural yogurt, add 1 teaspoon French mustard and 1 tablespoon lemon juice and season well with salt and pepper. Pour the dressing over the salad vegetables and mix well. If liked, you could add 40 g/1½ oz raisins and the same amount of chopped walnuts. Serve the coleslaw garnished with a sprinkling of chopped fresh mixed herbs. Serves 4.

Chapter 7
Teatime Treats

Victoria Sponge Cake

Serves 8–10

ingredients
- 175 g/6 oz butter, at room temperature, plus extra for greasing
- 175 g/6 oz caster sugar
- 3 eggs, beaten
- 175 g/6 oz self-raising flour
- pinch of salt
- 3 tbsp raspberry jam
- 1 tbsp caster sugar or icing sugar, for sprinkling

1 Preheat the oven to 180ºC/350ºF/ Gas Mark 4.

2 Grease two 20-cm/8-inch round cake tins and line with greaseproof paper or baking paper.

3 Cream the butter and sugar together in a mixing bowl using a wooden spoon or a hand-held mixer until the mixture is pale in colour and light and fluffy.

4 Add the eggs a little at a time, beating well after each addition.

5 Sift the flour and salt and carefully add to the mixture, folding it in with a metal spoon or a spatula.

6 Divide the mixture between the tins and smooth over with the spatula.

7 Place them on the same shelf in the centre of the oven and bake for 25–30 minutes until well risen, golden brown and beginning to shrink from the sides of the tin.

8 Remove from the oven and leave to stand for 1 minute. Loosen the cakes from around the edge of the tins using a palette knife. Turn the cakes out onto a clean tea towel, remove the paper and invert them onto a wire rack (this prevents the wire rack marking the top of the cakes).

9 When completely cool, sandwich together with the jam and sprinkle with the sugar. The cake is delicious when freshly baked, but any remaining cake can be stored in an airtight tin for up to 1 week.

Date & Walnut Teabread

Serves 8

ingredients

- 100 g/3½ oz stoned dates, chopped
- ½ tsp bicarbonate of soda
- finely grated rind of ½ lemon
- 100 ml/3½ fl oz hot tea
- 40 g/1½ oz unsalted butter, plus extra for greasing
- 70 g/2½ oz light muscovado sugar
- 1 small egg
- 125 g/4½ oz self-raising flour
- 25 g/1 oz walnuts, chopped
- walnut halves, to decorate

1 Preheat the oven to 180°C/350°F/ Gas Mark 4. Grease a 450-g/1-lb loaf tin and line the base with non-stick baking paper. Place the dates, bicarbonate of soda and lemon rind in a bowl and add the hot tea. Leave to soak for 10 minutes, until soft.

2 Cream together the butter and sugar until light and fluffy, then beat in the egg. Stir in the date mixture.

3 Fold in the flour using a large metal spoon, then fold in the walnuts. Spoon the mixture into the prepared cake tin and spread evenly. Top with walnut halves.

4 Bake in the preheated oven for 35–40 minutes, or until risen, firm and golden brown. Leave to cool for 10 minutes in the tin, then turn out the loaf and finish cooling on a wire rack.

Gingerbread

Serves 9

ingredients

- 175 g/6 oz unsalted butter, plus extra for greasing
- 150 g/5½ oz dark muscovado sugar
- 175 g/6 oz golden syrup
- finely grated rind and juice of 1 small orange
- 2 large eggs, beaten
- 225 g/8 oz self-raising flour
- 100 g/3½ oz plain wholemeal flour
- 2 tsp ground ginger
- 40 g/1½ oz chopped glacé ginger or stem ginger
- pieces of glacé ginger or stem ginger, to decorate

1 Preheat the oven to 180°C/350°F/ Gas Mark 4. Grease a 23-cm/9-inch square deep cake tin and line the base with non-stick baking paper.

2 Place the butter, sugar and golden syrup in a saucepan and heat gently, stirring until melted. Remove from the heat.

3 Beat in the orange rind and juice, eggs, self-raising flour, wholemeal flour and ground ginger, then beat thoroughly to mix evenly. Stir in the glacé ginger.

4 Spoon the batter into the prepared tin and bake in the preheated oven for 40–45 minutes, or until risen and firm to the touch.

5 Leave to cool in the tin for about 10 minutes, then turn out and finish cooling on a wire rack. Cut into squares and decorate with some glacé ginger.

Battenberg Cake

Serves 6–8

ingredients

- 115 g/4 oz butter or margarine, softened, plus extra for greasing
- 115 g/4 oz caster sugar, plus extra for sprinkling
- 2 eggs, lightly beaten
- 1 tsp vanilla extract
- 115 g/4 oz self-raising flour, sifted
- a few drops of pink food colouring
- 2–3 tbsp apricot jam
- 300 g/10½ oz marzipan

1 Preheat the oven to 180°C/350°F/ Gas Mark 4. Grease and line an 18-cm/7-inch shallow square baking tin. Cut a strip of double baking paper and grease it. Use this to divide the tin in half.

2 Cream the butter and sugar in a mixing bowl until pale and fluffy. Gently beat in the eggs and vanilla extract, gradually adding in the flour. Spoon half the mixture into a separate bowl and colour it with a few drops of food colouring.

3 Spoon the plain mixture into half the prepared baking tin. Spoon the coloured mixture into the other half of the tin, trying to make the divide as straight as possible. Bake in the preheated oven for 35–40 minutes. Turn out and leave to cool on a wire rack.

4 When cool, trim the edges and cut the cake portions lengthways in half, making four equal parts. Warm the jam in a small saucepan. Brush two sides of each cake portion with some jam and stick them together to give a chequerboard effect.

5 Knead the marzipan with a few drops of food colouring to colour it a subtle shade of pink. Roll out the marzipan to a rectangle wide enough to wrap around the cake. Brush the outside of the cake with the remaining jam. Place the cake on the marzipan and wrap the marzipan around the cake, making sure that the seam is on one corner of the cake. Trim the edges neatly. Crimp the top edges of the cake, if desired, and sprinkle with sugar.

Shortbread

Makes 8

ingredients

- 175 g/6 oz plain flour,
  plus extra for dusting
- pinch of salt
- 55 g/2 oz caster sugar,
  plus extra for sprinkling
- 115 g/4 oz butter, cut into small
  pieces, plus extra for greasing

1 Preheat the oven to 150°C/300°F/
Gas Mark 2. Grease a 20-cm/8-inch
fluted round tart tin.

2 Mix together the flour, salt and sugar.
Rub the butter into the dry ingredients.
Continue to work the mixture until it forms a
soft dough. Make sure you do not overwork
the shortbread or it will be tough, rather
than crumbly.

3 Lightly press the dough into the
prepared tart tin. Mark into eight
wedge-shaped pieces with a knife.
Prick all over with a fork and bake in the
preheated oven for 45–50 minutes, until the
shortbread is firm and just coloured.

4 Leave to cool in the tin and sprinkle with
the sugar. Cut into portions and place
on a wire rack to cool completely.

Scones

Makes 10–12

ingredients
- 450 g/1 lb plain flour, plus extra for dusting
- ½ tsp salt
- 2 tsp baking powder
- 55 g/2 oz butter
- 2 tbsp caster sugar
- 250 ml/9 fl oz milk, plus extra for brushing
- Raspberry Jam (see page 192) and clotted cream, to serve

1 Preheat the oven to 220°C/425°F/ Gas Mark 7.

2 Sift the flour, salt and baking powder into a bowl. Rub in the butter using your fingertips until the mixture resembles breadcrumbs. Stir in the sugar. Make a well in the centre and pour in the milk. Stir in using a palette knife and bring together to make a soft dough.

3 Turn out the mixture onto a floured work surface and lightly flatten the dough until it is of an even thickness, about 1 cm/½ inch.

4 Cut out the scones using a 6-cm/2½-inch biscuit cutter and place on a baking tray.

5 Brush with a little milk and bake in the preheated oven for 10–12 minutes, until golden and well risen. Cool on a wire rack and serve freshly baked with Raspberry Jam and clotted cream.

Tea Cakes

Makes 10–12

ingredients
- 300 ml/10 fl oz milk
- 4 tsp dried yeast
- 55 g/2 oz caster sugar
- 450 g/1 lb strong white flour
- 1 tsp salt
- 1 tsp ground mixed spice
- 115 g/4 oz currants
- 25 g/1 oz mixed peel, chopped
- 55 g/2 oz butter, melted
- 1 egg, beaten
- sugar glaze made from 2 tbsp sugar and 2 tbsp warm milk

1 Put the milk in a saucepan and heat until just lukewarm. Add the yeast with 1 teaspoon of the sugar, mix well and leave to froth in a warm place for 15 minutes.

2 Sift the flour, salt and spice into a large mixing bowl and add the currants, mixed peel and the remaining sugar.

3 Make a well in the centre of the dry ingredients and pour in the milk mixture, melted butter and the egg.

4 Mix well using a wooden spoon at first and then by hand.

5 Turn out onto a lightly floured work surface and knead lightly until the dough is smooth and elastic.

6 Put the dough back into the bowl, cover with clingfilm and leave to rise in a warm place for 40–45 minutes until it has doubled in size.

7 Knead the dough again lightly and divide into 10–12 even-sized buns, shaping well.

8 Preheat the oven to 220ºC/425ºF/ Gas Mark 7. Place the buns on two greased baking trays, cover with a damp tea towel or large polythene bags and leave to rise again for 30–40 minutes.

9 Bake the tea cakes in the preheated oven for 18–20 minutes until they are golden brown. Remove from the oven, place on a wire rack and glaze with the sugar glaze while still hot.

Muffins

Makes 10–12

ingredients
- 2 x 7 g/⅛ oz sachets easy-blend dried yeast
- 250 ml/9 fl oz lukewarm water
- 125 ml/4 fl oz natural yogurt
- 450 g/1 lb strong white flour
- ½ tsp salt
- 50 g/1¼ oz fine semolina
- oil, for greasing
- butter and jam, to serve

1 Mix the yeast with half the water in a bowl until it has dissolved.

2 Add the remaining water and the yogurt and mix well.

3 Sift the flour into a large bowl and add the salt. Pour in the yeast liquid and mix well to a soft dough.

4 Turn out the dough onto a floured work surface and knead well until very smooth. Put back into the bowl, cover with clingfilm and leave to rise for 30–40 minutes in a warm place until it has doubled in size.

5 Turn out again onto the work surface and knead lightly. Roll out the dough to a thickness of 2 cm/¾ inch.

6 Using a 7.5-cm/3-inch cutter, cut into rounds and scatter the semolina over each muffin. Re-roll the trimmings of the dough and use to make more muffins. Place the muffins on a lightly floured baking tray, cover and leave to rise again for 30–40 minutes.

7 Heat a griddle or a large frying pan and lightly grease with a little oil. Cook half the muffins for 7–8 minutes on each side, taking care not to burn them. Repeat with the rest of the muffins.

8 Serve freshly cooked with lots of butter. Muffins can be kept for two days in an airtight tin. To reheat, split them across the centre and quickly toast them before serving with butter and jam.

Crumpets

Makes 10–12

ingredients

- 350 g/12 oz plain flour
- pinch of salt
- 15 g/½ oz fresh yeast
- 1 tsp caster sugar
- 400 ml/14 fl oz lukewarm milk
- butter, to serve

1 Place the flour and salt in a mixing bowl and mix together. Blend the yeast with the sugar in a bowl and add the milk.

2 Pour the liquid onto the flour and mix everything together until the batter is smooth, beating it thoroughly so that it is light and airy. Cover and leave to rise in a warm place for 1 hour until well risen.

3 Stir the batter to knock out any air and check the consistency. If it is too thick, add 1 tablespoon of water (it should look rather gloopy). Set aside for 10 minutes.

4 Grease the frying pan and four crumpet rings or 7.5-cm/3-inch plain cutters. Heat the pan over a medium heat for 2 minutes. Arrange the rings in the pan and spoon in enough batter to come halfway up each ring. Cook over a low heat for 5–6 minutes until small holes appear and the top is starting to dry.

5 Remove the crumpet rings with a palette knife or an oven glove. Turn the crumpets over (the base should be golden brown) and cook the top for just 1–2 minutes to cook through.

6 Keep the first batch of crumpets warm while you cook the rest of the batter.

7 Serve freshly cooked with butter or, if you want to serve them later, leave them to cool and reheat in a toaster or by the fire.

Barm Brack

Makes 1 loaf

ingredients

- 650 g/1 lb 7 oz strong white flour, plus extra for dusting
- 1 tsp mixed spice
- 1 tsp salt
- 2 tsp easy-blend dried yeast
- 1 tbsp golden caster sugar
- 300 ml/10 fl oz lukewarm milk
- 150 ml/5 fl oz lukewarm water
- vegetable oil, for oiling
- 4 tbsp softened butter, plus extra to serve
- 325 g/11½ oz mixed dried fruit (sultanas, currants and raisins)
- milk, for glazing
- butter, to serve

1 Sift the flour, mixed spice and salt into a warmed bowl. Stir in the yeast and caster sugar. Make a well in the centre and pour in the milk and water. Mix well to make a sticky dough. Turn out the dough onto a lightly floured surface and knead until no longer sticky. Put into an oiled bowl, cover with clingfilm and leave to rise in a warm place for 1 hour until doubled in size.

2 Turn out the dough onto a floured work surface and knead lightly for 1 minute. Add the butter and dried fruit to the dough and work them in until completely incorporated. Return the dough to the bowl, replace the clingfilm and leave to rise for 30 minutes.

3 Oil a 23-cm/9-inch round cake tin. Pat the dough to a neat round and fit it into the tin. Cover and leave in a warm place until the dough has risen to the top of the tin. Meanwhile, preheat the oven to 200°C/400°F/Gas Mark 6.

4 Brush the top of the loaf lightly with milk and bake in the preheated oven for 15 minutes. Cover the loaf with foil, reduce the oven temperature to 180°C/350°F/Gas Mark 4 and bake for a further 45 minutes until it is golden brown and sounds hollow when tapped on the base. Transfer to a wire rack and leave to cool. Serve, sliced, with butter.

Irish Soda Bread

Serves 4–6

ingredients
• 450 g/1 lb plain flour
• 1 tsp salt
• 1 tsp bicarbonate of soda
• 400 ml/14 fl oz buttermilk

1 Preheat the oven to 220ºC/425ºF/ Gas Mark 7.

2 Sift the flour, salt and bicarbonate of soda into a mixing bowl.

3 Make a well in the centre of the dry ingredients and pour in most of the buttermilk. Mix well together using your hands. The dough should be very soft but not too wet. If necessary, add the remaining buttermilk.

4 Turn out the dough onto a lightly floured work surface and knead lightly. Shape into a 20-cm/8-inch round.

5 Place the bread on a greased baking tray, cut a cross in the top and bake in the preheated oven for 25–30 minutes. When done it should sound hollow if tapped on the base. Eat while still warm. Soda bread is always best eaten on the day it is made.

Raspberry Jam

Makes 5 x 450 g/1 lb jars

ingredients
- 1.3 kg/3 lb raspberries
- 1.3 kg/3 lb granulated or preserving sugar

1 You will need five 450 g/1 lb jam jars with lids and waxed discs. To sterilize the jars, wash them in soapy water, rinse well and place in a moderate oven for 5 minutes.

2 Put the fruit into a large saucepan and slowly cook until some of the juices begin to run. Simmer gently for 15–20 minutes until tender. Add the sugar and stir until dissolved.

3 Raise the heat and boil hard for 2–3 minutes until setting point is reached. Test if the jam is set by using a sugar thermometer. When it reads 105°C/221°F it is at a good setting point.

4 Remove the pan from the heat and leave to cool for 2 minutes, skimming if necessary.

5 Fill the warmed jars carefully using a ladle and a jam funnel. Top with the waxed discs and screw on the lids. Wipe the jars clean and leave to cool. Label and date to avoid confusion later.

6 Store in a cool, dry place. Once opened the jam will keep for up to 2 months in the refrigerator.

Lemon Curd

Makes 700 g/1 lb 9 oz

ingredients
- 3 unwaxed lemons
- 350 g/12 oz caster sugar
- 3 eggs, beaten
- 175 g/6 oz butter, cut into small pieces

1 You will need three or four small jars with lids and waxed discs. To sterilize the jars, wash them in soapy water, rinse well, then place in a moderate oven for 5 minutes.

2 Carefully grate the rind from each of the lemons using a fine grater. Make sure you take only the yellow rind and not the bitter white pith.

3 Halve the lemons, squeeze out all the juice and strain to remove the pips.

4 Place a medium-sized heatproof bowl over a saucepan of simmering water and add the lemon rind, juice and sugar. Mix together well until the sugar has dissolved.

5 Add the eggs and the butter and continue to stir for 25–30 minutes until the butter has melted and the mixture begins to thicken. Beat well and turn into the jars. Cover and label before storing. Once opened the lemon curd will keep for up to 2 months in the refrigerator.

Chapter 8
Puddings

Apple Pie

Serves 6

ingredients
- 750 g–1 kg/1 lb 10 oz–2 lb 4 oz cooking apples, peeled, cored and sliced
- 125 g/4½ oz soft light brown sugar or caster sugar, plus extra for sprinkling
- ½–1 tsp ground cinnamon, mixed spice or ground ginger
- 1–2 tbsp water (optional)

pastry
- 350 g/12 oz plain flour
- pinch of salt
- 85 g/3 oz butter or margarine, cut into small pieces
- 85 g/3 oz lard or white vegetable fat, cut into small pieces
- about 6 tbsp cold water
- beaten egg or milk, for glazing

1 To make the pastry, sift the flour and salt into a mixing bowl. Add the butter and lard and rub in with your fingertips until the mixture resembles fine breadcrumbs. Add the water and gather the mixture together into a dough. Wrap the dough and chill in the refrigerator for 30 minutes.

2 Preheat the oven to 220°C/425°F/ Gas Mark 7. Thinly roll out almost two thirds of the pastry and use to line a deep 23-cm/9-inch pie plate or pie tin.

3 Mix the apples with the sugar and spice and pack into the pastry case. Add the water if needed, particularly if the apples are not very juicy.

4 Roll out the remaining pastry to form a lid. Dampen the edges of the pie rim with water and position the lid, pressing the edges firmly together, then trim and crimp the edges.

5 Using the trimmings, cut out leaves or other shapes to decorate the top of the pie. Dampen and attach. Glaze the top of the pie with beaten egg or milk, make one or two slits in the top and place the pie on a baking tray.

6 Bake in the preheated oven for 20 minutes, then reduce the oven temperature to 180°C/350°F/ Gas Mark 4 and bake for a further 30 minutes, or until the pastry is a light golden brown. Serve hot or cold, sprinkled with sugar.

Lemon Meringue Pie

Serves 6–8

ingredients

pastry

- 150 g/5½ oz plain flour, plus extra for dusting
- 85 g/3 oz butter, cut into small pieces, plus extra for greasing
- 35 g/1¼ oz icing sugar, sifted
- finely grated rind of ½ lemon
- ½ egg yolk, beaten
- 1½ tbsp milk

filling

- 3 tbsp cornflour
- 300 ml/10 fl oz water
- juice and grated rind of 2 lemons
- 175 g/6 oz caster sugar
- 2 eggs, separated

1 To make the pastry, sift the flour into a bowl. Rub in the butter with your fingertips until the mixture resembles fine breadcrumbs. Mix in the remaining ingredients. Turn out onto a lightly floured work surface and knead briefly. Wrap in clingfilm and chill in the refrigerator for 30 minutes.

2 Preheat the oven to 180°C/350°F/ Gas Mark 4. Grease a 20-cm/8-inch round tart tin. Roll out the pastry to a thickness of 5 mm/¼ inch, then use it to line the base and sides of the tin. Prick all over with a fork, line with baking paper and fill with baking beans. Bake in the preheated oven for 15 minutes. Remove the pastry case from the oven and take out the paper and beans. Reduce the temperature to 150°C/300°F/Gas Mark 2.

3 For the filling, mix the cornflour with a little of the water to form a paste. Put the remaining water in a saucepan. Stir in the lemon juice and rind and the cornflour paste. Bring to the boil, stirring. Cook for 2 minutes. Leave to cool a little. Stir in 5 tablespoons of the caster sugar and the egg yolks, and pour into the pastry case.

4 Whisk the egg whites in a clean, grease-free bowl until stiff. Gradually whisk in the remaining caster sugar and spread over the pie. Return the pie to the oven and bake for a further 40 minutes. Remove from the oven and leave to cool before serving.

Treacle Tart

Serves 8

ingredients

- 250 g/ 9 oz ready-made shortcrust pastry
- plain flour, for dusting
- 350 g/12 oz golden syrup
- 125 g/4½ oz fresh white breadcrumbs
- 125 ml/4 fl oz double cream
- finely grated rind of ½ lemon or orange
- 2 tbsp lemon juice or orange juice
- whipped cream or clotted cream, to serve

1 Roll out the pastry on a lightly floured work surface and use to line a 20-cm/8-inch round loose-based tart tin, reserving the pastry trimmings. Prick the base of the pastry case all over with a fork, cover with clingfilm and chill in the refrigerator for 30 minutes. Re-roll the reserved pastry trimmings and cut out small shapes, such as leaves, stars or hearts, to decorate the top of the tart.

2 Preheat the oven to 190°C/375°F/ Gas Mark 5.

3 Mix the golden syrup, breadcrumbs, double cream and lemon rind with the lemon juice in a small bowl. Pour the mixture into the pastry case and decorate the top of the tart with the pastry shapes.

4 Transfer to the preheated oven and bake for 35–40 minutes, or until the filling is just set.

5 Leave the tart to cool slightly in the tin, then turn out and serve with cream.

Rhubarb Crumble

Serves 6

ingredients
- 900 g/2 lb rhubarb
- 115 g/4 oz caster sugar
- grated rind and juice of 1 orange
- cream, yogurt or custard, to serve

crumble topping
- 225 g/8 oz plain flour or wholemeal flour
- 115 g/4 oz unsalted butter
- 115 g/4 oz soft light brown sugar
- 1 tsp ground ginger

1 Preheat the oven to 190°C/375°F/ Gas Mark 5. Cut the rhubarb into 2.5-cm/1-inch lengths and place in a 1.7-litre/3-pint ovenproof dish with the sugar and the orange rind and juice.

2 Make the crumble topping by placing the flour in a mixing bowl and rubbing in the unsalted butter until the mixture resembles breadcrumbs. Stir in the sugar and the ginger.

3 Spread the crumble evenly over the fruit and press down lightly using a fork. Bake in the centre of the preheated oven on a baking tray for 25–30 minutes until the crumble is golden brown. Serve warm, accompanied with cream.

Spotted Dick & Custard

Serves 6

ingredients
- 225 g/8 oz self-raising flour
- 115 g/4 oz suet
- 55 g/2 oz caster sugar
- 140 g/5 oz currants or raisins
- grated rind of 1 lemon
- 150–175 ml/5–6 fl oz milk
- 2 tsp melted butter, for greasing

custard
- 425 ml/15 fl oz single cream
- 5 egg yolks
- 3 tbsp caster sugar
- ½ tsp vanilla extract
- 1 tsp cornflour (optional)

1 Put the flour, suet, sugar, currants and lemon rind into a mixing bowl and mix together well.

2 Pour in the milk and stir to give a fairly soft dough.

3 Turn out the dough onto a floured surface and roll into a cylinder. Wrap in greaseproof paper that has been well-buttered and seal the ends, leaving room for the pudding to rise. Over-wrap with foil and place in a steamer over a saucepan of boiling water.

4 Steam for about 1–1½ hours, checking the water level in the saucepan from time to time.

5 To make the custard, heat the cream in a small saucepan just to boiling point. Cream the egg yolks, sugar and vanilla extract together in a measuring jug. You can add the cornflour to this cold egg yolk mixture to ensure the sauce does not separate. Pour the hot cream into the jug, stirring all the time. Return the mixture to the saucepan.

6 Heat the custard very gently, stirring constantly, until the sauce has just thickened, then remove from the heat. Alternatively, you can cook the custard in a bowl over a saucepan of simmering water to prevent overcooking.

7 Remove the pudding from the steamer and unwrap. Place on a hot plate and cut into thick slices. Serve with lots of custard for pouring over.

Baked Rice Pudding

Serves 4–6

ingredients
- 1 tbsp melted unsalted butter
- 115 g/4 oz pudding rice
- 55 g/2 oz caster sugar
- 850 ml/1½ pints milk
- ½ tsp vanilla extract
- 40 g/1½ oz unsalted butter, chilled and cut into pieces
- whole nutmeg, for grating
- cream, jam, fresh fruit purée, stewed fruit, honey or ice cream, to serve

1 Preheat the oven to 150ºC/300ºF/ Gas Mark 2. Grease a 1.2-litre/2-pint baking dish (a gratin dish is good) with the melted butter, place the rice in the dish and sprinkle with the sugar.

2 Heat the milk in a saucepan until almost boiling, then pour over the rice. Add the vanilla extract and stir well to dissolve the sugar.

3 Cut the butter into small pieces and scatter over the surface of the pudding.

4 Grate the whole nutmeg over the top, using as much as you like to give a good covering.

5 Place the dish on a baking tray and bake in the centre of the preheated oven for 1½–2 hours until the pudding is well browned on the top. You can stir it after the first half hour to disperse the rice.

6 Serve hot topped with cream, jam, fresh fruit purée, stewed fruit, honey or ice cream.

Bread & Butter Pudding

Serves 4–6

ingredients

- 85 g/3 oz butter, softened
- 6 slices thick white bread
- 55 g/2 oz mixed fruit (sultanas, currants and raisins)
- 25 g/1 oz candied peel
- 3 large eggs
- 300 ml/10 fl oz milk
- 150 ml/5 fl oz double cream
- 55 g/2 oz caster sugar
- whole nutmeg, for grating
- 1 tbsp demerara sugar
- cream, to serve

1 Preheat the oven to 180°C/350°F/ Gas Mark 4.

2 Use a little of the butter to grease a 20 x 25-cm/8 x 10-inch baking dish and the remainder to butter the slices of bread. Cut the bread slices into quarters and arrange half overlapping in the dish.

3 Scatter half the dried fruit and candied peel over the bread, cover with the remaining bread slices and add the remaining fruit and peel.

4 In a mixing jug, whisk the eggs well and mix in the milk, cream and sugar. Pour this over the pudding and leave to stand for 15 minutes to allow the bread to soak up some of the egg mixture. Tuck in most of the fruit as you do not want it to burn in the oven. Grate the nutmeg over the top of the pudding, according to taste, and sprinkle over the demerara sugar.

5 Place the pudding on a baking tray and bake at the top of the preheated oven for 30–40 minutes until just set and golden brown.

6 Remove from the oven and serve warm with a little pouring cream.

Jam Roly-poly

Serves 6

ingredients
- 225 g/8 oz self-raising flour
- pinch of salt
- 115 g/4 oz suet
- grated rind of 1 lemon
- 1 tbsp sugar
- 125 ml/4 fl oz mixed milk and water
- 4–6 tbsp strawberry jam
- 2 tablespoons milk
- Custard (see page 207), to serve

1 Sift the flour into a mixing bowl and add the salt and suet. Mix together well. Stir in the lemon rind and the sugar.

2 Make a well in the centre and add the liquid to give a light, elastic dough. Knead lightly until smooth. If you have time, wrap the dough in clingfilm and leave to rest for 30 minutes.

3 Roll the dough into a 20 x 25-cm/ 8 x 10-inch rectangle. Spread the jam over the dough, leaving a 1 cm/½ inch border. Brush the border with the milk and roll up the dough carefully, like a Swiss roll, from one short end. Seal the ends.

4 Wrap the roly-poly loosely in some greaseproof paper and then in foil, sealing the ends well.

5 Prepare a steamer by half filling it with water and putting it on to boil. Place the roly-poly in the steamer and steam over rapidly boiling water for 1½–2 hours, making sure you top up the water from time to time.

6 When cooked, remove the roly-poly from the steamer, unwrap and serve, cut into slices, on a warmed plate, with some custard.

Steamed Syrup Sponge

Serves 6

ingredients
- butter, for greasing
- 2 tbsp golden syrup, plus extra to serve
- 115 g/4 oz butter
- 115 g/4 oz caster sugar
- 2 eggs, lightly beaten
- 175 g/6 oz self-raising flour
- 2 tbsp milk
- grated rind of 1 lemon

1 Butter a 1.2-litre/2-pint pudding basin and put the syrup into the bottom.

2 Beat the butter and sugar together until soft and creamy, then beat in the eggs, a little at a time.

3 Fold in the flour and stir in the milk to make a soft dropping consistency. Add the lemon rind. Turn the mixture into the pudding basin.

4 Cover the surface with a circle of greaseproof paper or baking paper and top with a pleated sheet of foil. Secure with some string or crimp the edges of the foil to ensure a tight fit around the basin.

5 Place the pudding in a large saucepan half-filled with boiling water. Cover the saucepan and bring back to the boil over a medium heat. Reduce the heat to a slow simmer and steam for 1½ hours until risen and firm. Keep checking the water level and top up with boiling water as necessary.

6 Remove the pan from the heat and lift out the pudding basin. Remove the cover and loosen the pudding from the sides of the basin using a knife.

7 Turn out into a warmed dish and heat a little more syrup for pouring over the pudding before serving.

Summer Pudding

Serves 6

ingredients
- 675 g/1 lb 8 oz mixed soft fruits, such as redcurrants, blackcurrants, raspberries and blackberries
- 140 g/5 oz caster sugar
- 2 tbsp crème de framboise liqueur (optional)
- 6–8 slices good day-old white bread, crusts removed
- icing sugar, for dusting (optional)
- double cream, to serve

1 Place the fruits in a large saucepan with the sugar.

2 Over a low heat, very slowly bring to the boil, stirring carefully to ensure that the sugar has dissolved. Cook over a low heat for 2–3 minutes until the juices run but the fruit still holds its shape. Add the liqueur, if using.

3 Line an 850-ml/1½-pint pudding basin with some of the slices of bread (cut them to shape so that the bread fits well). Spoon in the cooked fruit and juices, reserving a little of the juice for later.

4 Cover the surface of the fruit with the remaining bread. Place a saucer on top of the pudding, weight it and leave for at least 8 hours or overnight in the refrigerator.

5 Turn out the pudding and pour over the reserved juices to colour any white bits of bread that may be showing. Sprinkle with the icing sugar, if using, and serve with cream.

Classic Sherry Trifle

Serves 6–8

ingredients

- 8 trifle sponges or 1 layer of Victoria Sponge Cake (see page 171)
- 115 g/4 oz Raspberry Jam (see page 192)
- 150 ml/5 fl oz sherry
- 55 g/2 oz small macaroons or ratafia biscuits
- 2 tbsp brandy
- 350 g/12 oz raspberries, fresh or frozen
- 600 ml/1 pint Custard (see page 207), cooled
- 300 ml/10 fl oz double cream
- 2 tbsp milk
- 40 g/1½ oz toasted flaked almonds or silver dragées, to decorate

1 Break the sponges or cake into pieces and spread with the jam.

2 Place in a large glass serving bowl and pour over the sherry. Add the macaroons to the bowl and sprinkle over the brandy.

3 Spoon the raspberries on top. Pour over the custard, cover the bowl with clingfilm and leave to settle for 2–3 hours or overnight.

4 Just before serving, whip the cream with the milk until it is thick but still soft. Spoon over the custard and swirl around using a knife to give an attractive appearance. Decorate with flaked almonds and serve.

apples
    apple pie 199
    apple sauce 127
    apple & spice porridge 23
    boned & stuffed roast
        duck 107
    braised red cabbage 159
    celery & walnut stuffing 103
    coleslaw 167
    pork & apple pie 65
apricots
    boned & stuffed roast
        duck 107
    celery & walnut stuffing 103
    coronation chicken 70
asparagus with melted
    butter 164

bacon
    bacon butties 28
    chestnut stuffing 103
    the full English 27
    with laverbread 31
    mushroom risotto 153
    star-gazy pie 136
barm brack 15, 188
Battenberg cake 176
batter
    toad-in-the-hole 124
    vegetable toad-in-the-
        hole 90
    Yorkshire puddings 74
beef
    beef stew with herb
        dumplings 73
    beef Wellington 95
    Cornish pasties 62
    roast beef 119
    roast beef & horseradish
        sandwiches 53
    steak & kidney pie 77
berries
    summer pudding 216
    see also raspberries

bread
    bacon butties 28
    bread & butter pudding 211
    bread sauce 104
    broccoli & Stilton soup 45
    classic orange marmalade &
        toast 24
    classic sandwich selection 53
    the full English 27
    Irish soda bread 191
    summer pudding 216
    Welsh rarebit 57
bread sauce 104
breakfasts
    apple & spice porridge 23
    bacon butties 28
    baked eggs 35
    boiled eggs 32
    classic orange marmalade &
        toast 24
    fried eggs 35
    the full English 27
    kedgeree 40
    kippers 39
    laverbread 31
    poached eggs 35
    potato cakes 36
    scrambled eggs 32
broccoli & Stilton soup 45
Brussels sprouts with buttered
    chestnuts 151
bubble & squeak 155
butternut squash: roasted root
    vegetables 163

cabbage
    braised red cabbage 159
    bubble & squeak 155
    coleslaw 167
cakes
    Battenberg cake 176
    Victoria sponge cake 171

carrots
    braised lamb shanks 82
    coleslaw 167
    coronation chicken 70
    Irish stew 78
    ploughman's with
        chutney 54
    roasted root vegetables 163
    Scotch broth 49
    shepherd's pie 123
    vegetable toad-in-the-
        hole 90
cauliflower cheese 148
celebrations 10–12
celery
    braised lamb shanks 82
    celery & walnut stuffing 103
    Scotch broth 49
champ 144
cheese
    broccoli & Stilton soup 45
    cauliflower cheese 148
    pan haggerty 58
    perfect macaroni cheese 139
    ploughman's with chutney 54
    roasted onions 160
    smoked salmon & cream
        cheese sandwiches 53
    Welsh rarebit 57
chestnuts
    Brussels sprouts with buttered
        chestnuts 151
    chestnut stuffing 103
    game pie 99
chicken
    chicken, mushroom & tarragon
        pie 128
    coronation chicken 70
    roast chicken 131
coleslaw 167
Cornish pasties 62
coronation chicken 70

cranberries
cranberry sauce 104
mixed nut roast with cranberry
& red wine sauce 115
cream
bread & butter pudding 211
broccoli & Stilton soup 45
champ 144
classic sherry trifle 219
cullen skink 50
custard 207
fisherman's pie 89
prawn cocktail 69
treacle tart 203
crumpets 187
cucumber sandwiches 53
cullen skink 50
custard
classic sherry trifle 219
spotted dick & custard 207
date & walnut teabread 172
dried fruit
barm brack 15, 188
braised red cabbage 159
bread & butter pudding 211
spotted dick & custard 207
tea cakes 183
duck: boned & stuffed roast
duck 107

East Anglia 12–13
Easter eggs 11
eggs
baked eggs 35
Battenberg cake 176
boiled eggs 32
bread & butter pudding 211
custard 207
egg & cress sandwiches 53
fried eggs 35
the full English 27
gammon steaks with fried egg
& chips 85

gingerbread 175
ham & egg pie 61
hollandaise sauce 108
kedgeree 40
lemon curd 195
lemon meringue pie 200
ploughman's with chutney 54
poached eggs 35
scrambled eggs 32
star-gazy pie 136
steamed syrup sponge 215
toad-in-the-hole 124
vegetable toad-in-the-
hole 90
Victoria sponge cake 171
Yorkshire puddings 74

fish & seafood
cullen skink 50
fish cakes 135
fish & chips 132
fisherman's pie 89
griddled scallops with crispy
leeks 111
star-gazy pie 136
see also prawns; salmon;
smoked fish
fisherman's pie 89
French beans: vegetable toad-
in-the-hole 90

game pie 99
gammon
gammon steaks with fried egg
& chips 85
roast gammon 96
gingerbread 175
golden syrup
steamed syrup sponge 215
treacle tart 203
game pie 99
gravy 104

ham
ham & egg pie 61
ploughman's with chutney 54
see also gammon
herb dumplings 73
honeyed parsnips 147
hot cross buns 11

Irish soda bread 191
Irish stew 78
jam
classic sherry trifle 219
jam roly-poly 212
raspberry jam 192
Victoria sponge cake 171
kedgeree 40
kippers 39

lamb
braised lamb shanks 82
Irish stew 78
roast leg of lamb 120
Scotch broth 49
shepherd's pie 123
laverbread 31
leeks
griddled scallops with crispy
leeks 111
leek & potato soup 46
Scotch broth 49
lemons
chestnut stuffing 103
classic orange marmalade &
toast 24
lemon curd 195
lemon meringue pie 200
poached salmon with
hollandaise sauce 108
steamed syrup sponge 215
treacle tart 203
London and the South 16–17
macaroni pasta: perfect
macaroni cheese 139

marzipan: Battenberg cake 176
Midlands 13
muffins 184
mushrooms
    baked mushrooms 152
    beef Wellington 95
    chestnut stuffing 103
    chicken, mushroom & tarragon
        pie 128
    fisherman's pie 89
    the full English 27
    game pie 99
    mushroom risotto 153
    mushrooms in red wine 152

neeps & tatties 156
North of England 13–14
Northern Ireland 14–15
nuts
    mixed nut roast with cranberry
        & red wine sauce 115
    see also chestnuts; walnuts

oats, oatmeal
    apple & spice porridge 23
    laverbread 31
onions
    beef stew with herb
        dumplings 73
    braised lamb shanks 82
    braised red cabbage 159
    bread sauce 104
    broccoli & Stilton soup 45
    bubble & squeak 155
    celery & walnut stuffing 103
    chestnut stuffing 103
    chicken, mushroom & tarragon
        pie 128
    Cornish pasties 62
    coronation chicken 70
    cullen skink 50
    game pie 99

Irish stew 78
kedgeree 40
leek & potato soup 46
mixed nut roast with cranberry
    & red wine sauce 115
mushroom risotto 153
mushrooms in red wine 152
pan haggerty 58
pork & apple pie 65
pork hot pot 81
roasted onions 160
sausage & mash with onion
    gravy 86
Scotch broth 49
shepherd's pie 123
star-gazy pie 136
steak & kidney pie 77
vegetable toad-in-the-
    hole 90
venison casserole 100
oranges
    classic orange marmalade &
        toast 24
    gingerbread 175
    rhubarb crumble 204
    treacle tart 203
oven temperatures 224
oysters 10

pan haggerty 58
pancakes 10
parsnips
    honeyed parsnips 147
    roasted root vegetables 163
pastry
    apple pie 199
    beef Wellington 95
    chicken, mushroom & tarragon
        pie 128
    Cornish pasties 62
    game pie 99
    ham & egg pie 61

lemon meringue pie 200
    pork & apple pie 65
    star-gazy pie 136
    steak & kidney pie 77
    treacle tart 203
pearl barley: Scotch broth 49
peas: chicken, mushroom &
    tarragon pie 128
pine kernels: mixed nut roast
with cranberry & red wine
    sauce 115
ploughman's with chutney 54
pork
    pork hot pot 81
    roast pork with crackling 127
pork pie
    ploughman's with chutney 54
    pork & apple pie 65
potatoes
    broccoli & Stilton soup 45
    bubble & squeak 155
    champ 144
    Cornish pasties 62
    cullen skink 50
    fish cakes 135
    fish & chips 132
    fisherman's pie 89
    gammon steaks with fried egg
        & chips 85
    Irish stew 78
    leek & potato soup 46
    neeps & tatties 156
    pan haggerty 58
    perfect roast potatoes 143
    pork & apple pie 65
    potato cakes 36
    sausage & mash with onion
        gravy 86
    shepherd's pie 123
    special potato salad 167
prawns
    fisherman's pie 89
    garlic & herb Dublin Bay
        prawns 112

prawn cocktail 69
puddings
    apple pie 199
    baked rice pudding 208
    bread & butter pudding 211
    classic sherry trifle 219
    jam roly-poly 212
    lemon meringue pie 200
    rhubarb crumble 204
    spotted dick & custard 207
    steamed syrup sponge 215
    summer pudding 216
    treacle tart 203

raspberries
    classic sherry trifle 219
    raspberry jam 192
redcurrant jelly: braised red
    cabbage 159
regional cooking 12–18
rhubarb crumble 204
rice
    baked rice pudding 208
    kedgeree 40
    mushroom risotto 152

salad leaves
    ploughman's with chutney 54
    prawn cocktail 69
    simple garden salad 166
salads
    coleslaw 167
    simple garden salad 166
    special potato salad 167
    tomato salad 166
salmon
    poached salmon with
        hollandaise sauce 108
    smoked salmon & cream
        cheese sandwiches 53
sausages, sausage meat
    boned & stuffed roast

duck 107
    the full English 27
    sausage & mash with onion
        gravy 86
    toad-in-the-hole 124
scones 180
Scotch broth 49
Scotland 16
seasonal food 10, 19
shepherd's pie 123
shortbread 179
simnel cake 10–11
smoked fish
    cullen skink 50
    kedgeree 40
    kippers 39
    smoked salmon & cream
        cheese sandwiches 53
soups
    broccoli & Stilton soup 45
    cullen skink 50
    leek & potato soup 46
    Scotch broth 49
spinach: perfect macaroni
    cheese 139
spotted dick & custard 207
spring onions
    champ 144
    coleslaw 167
star-gazy pie 136
steak & kidney pie 77
suet
    herb dumplings 73
    jam roly-poly 212
    spotted dick & custard 207
summer pudding 216
swedes
    Cornish pasties 62
    neeps & tatties 156
sweet potatoes: roasted root
    vegetables 163
sweetcorn: vegetable toad-in-
    the-hole 90

tea cakes 183
teabreads
    date & walnut teabread 172
    gingerbread 175
toad-in-the-hole 124
tomatoes
    bacon butties 28
    with laverbread 31
    ploughman's with chutney 54
    pork hot pot 81
    tomato salad 166
    vegetable toad-in-the-
        hole 90
treacle tart 203
turkey: roast turkey with two
    stuffings 103
turnips
    roasted root vegetables 163
    Scotch broth 49

venison casserole 100
Victoria sponge cake 171
volume measures 224

Wales 17
walnuts
    boned & stuffed roast
        duck 107
    celery & walnut stuffing 103
    date & walnut teabread 172
    mixed nut roast with cranberry
        & red wine sauce 115
weight measures 224
Welsh rarebit 57
West Country 18

yogurt
    coleslaw 167
    coronation chicken 70
    muffins 184
Yorkshire puddings 74

Conversion Charts

temperatures

CELSIUS	GAS	FAHRENHEIT
110	¼	225
120	½	250
140	1	275
150	2	300
160	3	325
180	4	350
190	5	375
200	6	400
220	7	425
230	8	450
240	9	475

volume measures

METRIC	IMPERIAL
1.25 ML	¼ TSP
2.5 ML	½ TSP
5 ML	1 TSP
10 ML	2 TSP
15 ML	1 TBSP/3 TSP
30 ML	2 TBSP
45 ML	3 TBSP
60 ML	4 TBSP
75 ML	5 TBSP
90 ML	6 TBSP
15 ML	½ FL OZ
30 ML	1 FL OZ
50 ML	2 FL OZ
75 ML	2½ FL OZ
100 ML	3½ FL OZ
125 ML	4 FL OZ
150 ML	5 FL OZ
175 ML	6 FL OZ
200 ML	7 FL OZ
225 ML	8 FL OZ
250 ML	9 FL OZ
300 ML	10 FL OZ
350 ML	12 FL OZ
400 ML	14 FL OZ
425 ML	15 FL OZ
450 ML	16 FL OZ
500 ML	18 FL OZ
600 ML	1 PINT

weight measures

METRIC	IMPERIAL
5 G	⅛ OZ
10 G	¼ OZ
15 G	½ OZ
25/30 G	1 OZ
35 G	1¼ OZ
40 G	1½ OZ
50 G	1¾ OZ
55 G	2 OZ
60 G	2¼ OZ
70 G	2½ OZ
85 G	3 OZ
90 G	3¼ OZ
100 G	3½ OZ
115 G	4 OZ
125 G	4½ OZ
140 G	5 OZ
150 G	5½ OZ
175 G	6 OZ
200 G	7 OZ
225 G	8 OZ
250 G	9 OZ
275 G	9¾ OZ
280 G	10 OZ
300 G	10½ OZ
325 G	11½ OZ
350 G	12 OZ
375 G	13 OZ
400 G	14 OZ
425 G	15 OZ
450 G	1 LB
500 G	1 LB 2 OZ